BONNIE PRINCE
CHARLIE
AND THE '45

GEDDES&GROSSET

This edition published 2000 by Geddes & Grosset, an imprint
of Children's Leisure Products Limited

© 2000 Children's Leisure Products Limited, David Dale
House, New Lanark ML11 9DJ, Scotland

Adapted from a text by Grant R. Francis

ISBN 1 85534 900 0

Printed and bound in India

CONTENTS

CHAPTER I

*B*OYHOOD AND YOUTH

Charles Edward Stuart was the grandson of King James II and VII, who lost the throne of Britain to his daughter Mary and her Dutch husband, William of Orange, in 1688. Charles's father was James Francis Edward Stuart, known to Jacobites as 'King James the Third' and 'the Old Chevalier' and later dubbed the Old Pretender, the only son by his second wife, Mary of Modena, of James II. James Francis was born in London in June 1688, and in December of that year his mother took him to St Germains in France, a fugitive from William of Orange's victorious army. The young James was brought up in France, and when James II died in 1701 he was recognized as king of Great Britain and Ireland by France and Spain. In 1708 he made an abortive attempt to land in Scotland and returned to France to take part in the battles of Malplaquet and Oudenarde, fighting on the French side. Following the death in 1714 of the last Stuart monarch of Britain, Anne, and the succession of the Hanoverian George I, an unsuccessful attempt was made by the Jacobites in 1715 to set James on the throne of his ancestors by force. After the failure of this expedition, and under the terms of the Anglo-French Treaty of Utrecht, James was compelled to leave France and went to live in Rome under the auspices of the pope. There, in 1719, he married Maria Clementina, daughter of Prince James Sobieski of Poland and granddaughter of King John Sobieski.

Charles Edward Stuart was born on the night of 31 December 1720 in the Muti Palace in Rome, sixteen months after the marriage of his parents. It is said that a new star appeared in the heavens on the night of his birth, a sign that was regarded as an emblem of hope and promise by his father's supporters and was engraved on the medal that was subsequently struck in honour of the two young sons of the royal house. The motto on this medal, *alter ab illo* ('he shines before all'), also commemorates this celestial appearance on the night of his birth. The star was engraved on many of the Jacobite drinking glasses of the period, particularly those of the Cycle Club, which was presided over by Sir Watkyn Williams Wynn from

1724 onwards, and was often used as an emblem in conjunction with an oak leaf, which was commemorative of Charles II's restoration and indicative of the hope to see it repeated in the person of his great-nephew.

The young prince was given the names of Charles Edward Lewis John Casimir Silvester Maria Stuart. The names were carefully selected: Charles, on the advice of Lord Lansdowne that it was a name that 'is respected in England in memory of the first king of the name, and beloved in regard to the second'; Edward, as one of the greatest in English history; Lewis, in memory of the king of France who had been so constant a friend to his father's family; John and Casimir, by way of compliment to his mother's family; Silvester, because of his birth on Silvester Night, and Maria in memory of his grandmother, the devoted and faithful Queen Mary of Modena.

The next day 'King James' sent the usual advice to the courts of Europe that his 'queen' had given birth to a son, 'strong and robust, who is named Charles Edward'. He added a reminder in the letter to the Emperor of Austria, who had tried to prevent Clementina leaving Innsbruck to travel to Italy to marry James, that in spite of 'the measures Your Imperial Majesty had found it necessary formerly to take, the ties of blood and the justice of your heart will no doubt incline you to receive with pleasure the news that the Queen, your cousin, has borne me a Prince of Wales.'

The journalist and folklorist Andrew Lang quotes from a letter written in the spring of 1721 by a 'young English traveller of distinction, possibly Lord Rialton, afterwards Marquis of Blandford', who met the royal parents, 'the King in his Star and Garter, a well-sized, clean-limbed man resembling Charles II', and who states that he was presented by the royal command not only to the king and queen but also to the 'beautiful baby Prince of Wales'.

In 1724 Charles distinguished himself and pleased the Protestant Jacobites by declining to kneel to the new pope, Benedict XIII, when presented to him in the Vatican Gardens – remarkable precocity in a four-year-old infant who had already discovered the importance of being 'Prince of Wales'.

Two years later, the Duke of Wharton describes Charles in the following words: 'The Prince of Wales is one of the finest children I ever saw, and daily improves in body and mind by the care and assiduity of his present Governor,' Lord Dunbar.

Soon after this the Duke of Liria, a son of the Duke of Berwick who was a natural son of King James II and therefore the half-brother of James Francis and half-uncle of Charles, wrote similarly of him:

'The Prince of Wales is now six and a half, and besides his great beauty, is remarkable for dexterity, grace, and almost supernatural address. Not only can he read fluently, he can ride, fire a gun, and more surprising still, I have seen him take a crossbow and kill birds on the roof, and split a rolling ball ten times in succession. He speaks English, French, and Italian fluently, and altogether he is the most ideal Prince I have ever met in the course of my life.'

At this period of his life Andrew Lang describes the prince as 'a pretty boy with large *brown* eyes, and a smiling, happy, mischievous face, as in contemporary portraits'. It is probable that Lang is more or less right as to the colour of the eyes because they are given as brown in many contemporary paintings and engravings, but the point has been much disputed, as was also the case with Clementina, whom Lang described as having blue eyes.

The prince was eight years old at the time, and judging from a contemporary engraving by N. Edelinck of a painting by the French artist Antoine Davidde, he was certainly a most attractive and engaging child.

There is a curious and interesting feature in the engraving that gives some insight into the politics of the time. Edelinck's original plate portrayed Charles as Davidde had painted him, 'in his own hair' and without any headdress, and most remaining copies of the print are made from this original plate. It would appear probable, however, that because of the immense propaganda that was generated for a visit he made to Britain in 1750 this plate was used again, and the bonnet seen in this later impression was drawn in to indicate his connections with Scotland even in his childhood. The original line of the hair can still be traced under the re-engraving of the bonnet, which is in itself interesting as it is line for line exactly the same as another in a much later engraving, which is also attributable to 1750 and which is believed to be by Sir Robert Strange, although not published in that artist's list of works. Is it possible that the bonnet was drawn in by Strange himself on to the old Edelinck plate?

Another impression made from the altered plate was discovered by Helen Farquhar in the portrait gallery of Cortachy Castle, the home of the Earls of Airlie. She described it as 'sent out before the '45 to those who had suffered in the '15 to revive interest and to show what the young prince was like', ac-

The Altered Plate

cording to the tradition of the house of Ogilvy. This tradition − like so many others − does not perhaps bear too close inspection. The original prints may have been sent out with that intent about the year 1730 when the plate was first engraved, but certainly not in the altered state for the reason given above, i.e. that the bonnet is identical with that on an engraving of about 1750 and was, without a doubt, added to the plate *after* the '45 attempt when, has been pointed out by one writer, 'the glamour of the Prince's attempt and the romance of his escape' had made Highland garb popular throughout Europe.

It is far more probable that the Cortachy Castle example was sent after the '45 as a souvenir in gratitude for the then Earl of Airlie's loyal adherence to his prince and that the impression printed here had a similar origin, although the name of its recipient has been lost.

This early print is not coloured and therefore gives no help as to the colour of Charles' eyes, but another representation, and the best engraving of the prince at the height of his career, from a picture painted by Louis Tocque and engraved by J. G. Wille in Paris in 1748, is in colour and represents the eyes as grey-blue, like his mother's. Again, a snuffbox, prepared also for 1750 propaganda, contains a secret coloured miniature in the lid in which the eyes are a sort of hazel-grey. It is probable that this is nearer the truth, that they were of that curious hazel hue that shows almost grey-blue in some lights, but with a golden-brown tinge in others. This would account for the curious inconsistency of varying colours as shown on so many contemporary portraits.

In 1729 James records his comfort in his two sons (Henry had been born in 1725) and refers to Prince Charles as full of life and promise and something of a sportsman, the young prince having just shot his first hare.

Around that time in Rome, Baron Stosch was a Prussian spy of the English government who went under the name of John Walton. In his dispatches in 1731 this correspondent of the British ambassador constantly commented upon and regretted the impression created by the two young princes and the great attention paid to them by English travellers. He describes Prince Charles as 'the idol of his father's followers, full of life and hardihood, possessed of sense beyond his years, and of a very different temper from his father, likely to be much more popular than James had ever been' – a very true prophecy.

Incidentally, Andrew Lang admits that the same close observer of the prince, Stosch, or Walton, 'described Charles's eyes as blue', which is a contemporary contradiction of Lang's own description of them as brown and a confirmation of the probability suggested above that they were more hazel and grey than either brown or blue.

Lang frequently refers to John Walton's descriptions of the prince, every one to Charles's detriment, but these are so inaccurate, so obviously malicious and so biased against both the prince and his mother that beyond these brief references to them it is perhaps better to ignore them entirely.

As an example of these deliberate distortions of facts, at the time of the prince's birth Walton wrote, 'The child is so ill-fashioned that he would never be able to walk, and his mother could never be a mother again.' Both proved to be palpable lies, and as it is certain that Walton was paid to belittle and misrepresent facts for the consumption of the many disaffected English subjects, so it is surprising that Andrew Lang should appear to place such reliance on these as contemporary descriptions of the prince's character.

Other tributes to both the princes show how much they were admired. For example, James Murray, Earl of Dunbar and the Chevalier's secretary, writes to Lord Inverness:

'The Prince grows tall and strong and, as I believe, the most beautiful figure this day in the world, but . . . it is impossible to get him to apply to any study as he ought to do, or indeed to any tolerable degree, by which means the Latin goes ill on, but he speaks both French and Italian easily. The Duke [of York] . . . has all the lovely and great qualities that the most passionate of his friends could desire of him. Their Royal Highnesses were at a ball given them by Count Bologuetti. . . . I never saw in my life anything comparable to the beauty and grace with which the Prince appeared, and there were some English Whigs who could not conceal their emotion.'

It was, of course, an age of superlatives, but that this high tribute was not exaggerated is proved by a similar one from 'an English Whig', Samuel Crisp, who speaks in disparagement of the 'Pretender' but says of the two royal boys, 'they are two as fine youths as ever I saw, particularly the youngest who has more Beauty and Dignity in him than any one can form one's self an idea. He danced miraculously, as they say he does all his exercises, singing as I am told, most sweetly, and accompanying himself, and is in short the admiration of everybody.'

James, the fond father, pays Charles the following guarded tribute in a letter to Lord Inverness:

'There is no question of crushing the prince's spirit, and no danger of its being crushed, for he is mighty thoughtless and takes nothing much to heart; but I hope he will soon begin to think a little, and then with the natural parts God has given him, and the pains that are taken about him, I hope he will be good for something at last.'

How well the hope was to be fulfilled and how tragically it was all to be brought to nothing by the cruelties of a fate that he could not control.

In 1734 the prince, attended by Lord Dunbar and Sir Thomas Sheridan, saw his first military operation under the Duke of Liria, who had also just succeeded to his father's titles as Duke of Berwick and who was in command at the siege of Gaeta. The fact that he was going to his baptism of fire, under his father's old *nom de guerre* of 'the Chevalier de St George', was communicated for circulation in England. He was stated to have behaved at the Neapolitan Court 'with perfect ease, self-possession, and tactful good sense'.

He was just in time to be present at the fall of the beleaguered city and was eager to get into the forefront of the fighting. Lord Dunbar wrote of him when he got as far as an outpost where cannonballs had just fallen:

'This must be published in England. He talks to the Spanish soldiers in Spanish, to the Walloons in French, serves them with drink with his own hands, and they can talk of nothing else. He contrasts most favourably with the king of Naples.'

Here we see the beginning of the bonhomie and graciousness that were to carry him so far with subordinates in his later years.

His father, however, as always, had to remonstrate with him on the brevity of his badly spelled and ill-written letters – and well he might, for he received only two very short scrawls, while his brother, the Duke of York, who wrote to him frequently, and his anxious mother, received none at all.

The prince had a great reception in Naples, where he went when the campaign ended, and he returned with a reputation that, as Dunbar wrote to his father, 'so far outshone the King [of Naples] in the eyes of the public that it was natural that they should desire that an end might be put to the comparison between them.'

The Duke of Berwick was so delighted with his young kinsman's conduct and bearing that he wrote to his father offering to let the prince make a campaign with him whenever and wherever he pleased.

Soon after the prince's return he suffered the loss of

his young mother, and we can imagine his distress. The following year Lord Inverness, during a visit to Rome, wrote stating that he could not 'satisfy himself with admiring our two Princes, who are certainly the marvel of the world', but their father, with loving discrimination, qualifies this tribute with a regret that Charles is so 'wonderfully thoughtless for one of his age, though I hope a very little time will mend that'.

In the summer of 1737, Charles Edward made his first tour of Italy in the care of Lord Dunbar and Francis Strickland, thereafter closely connected with the prince until the Battle of Culloden. Charles travelled as the Count of Albany, a title that he was to use again in later life under less hopeful circumstances.

Some of the tributes paid to the gallant young prince during this tour throw considerable light on his character at the time. They are mostly drawn from the reports sent by Lord Dunbar to the 'king'. Thus, at Bologna he charmed everybody with his wonderful behaviour and the way he listened to speeches of welcome, and 'if Your Majesty could have seen the gravity with which the Prince heard these compositions I am sure you would have been diverted'.

Charles was, however, as poor at spelling as in his

later years, and the 'king' has to admonish him once more and to tell him to 'make a short meditation on your brother being four years younger than you are'. Dunbar also reports from Bologna that the prince will not dance with moderation but 'overheats himself monstrously, and sits too long at supper, so that it is not possible to get him to bed till three in the morning'.

At Venice he had a wonderful reception from the doge, and the Grand Council allotted him a place in the enclosure reserved for sovereign princes. Here he met the Elector of Bavaria and his wife, and was received as a relative by them in front of a large company, in which everyone remarked upon his 'air of superiority'. The English court was furious at his reception and sharply dismissed the Venetian representative because his country 'had thought fit to distinguish the son of the Pretender with very particular and extraordinary honours'.

Lang remarks that in August of the same year his long hair was now cut and that he wore a wig for the first time.

He appears at this time to have been a brilliant, somewhat unruly and high-spirited boy, already causing his governor some uneasiness by his fondness for the 'pleasures of the table' but free from all trace of other vices, as indeed he remained through-out his life. Like his father, women were less an attraction to him than attracted by him, and he was always more sought after than seeking in this respect. His unfortunate entanglement with Clementina Walkinshaw in later life was the only serious lapse in spite of the tolerance and loose habits of his age and station. His father even remarks upon his being 'very innocent and extremely backwards in some respects for his age'.

The first mention of religion in connection with Prince Charles Edward occurs in a letter in 1739 in which the princes are contrasted: 'The elder has much better parts, and a quicker apprehension than the younger, who, sensible of his inferiority in that respect, makes it up by greater application. The last is more lively, the other more considerate, both virtuous, both exceedingly good-natured and well-bred. The elder, who is more reasonable, and has the better knowledge and judgment, does not show any attachment to any particular mode of religion, to which the younger seems more disposed.'

In 1740 the French magistrate and writer Charles des Brosses visited Italy, and in *Letters from Italy*, first published in Paris in 1836, he paints an excellent word picture of the two princes:

'The elder is about twenty years of age, and the younger fifteen. They are amiable, polite, and gracious, but appear of moderate ability and less formed for their age than Princes ought to be. . . . I hear from those who know them that the elder is the favourite, that he has a good heart and great courage, feeling his position keenly, and that if he does not release himself from it, it will not be for lack of intrepidity. . . . Both Princes are passionately fond of music, and know it thoroughly; they have an exquisite concert once a week. . . . Yesterday I went in as they were playing Corelli's famous Concerto la Notte di Natale, and I expressed my regret at not having arrived in time to hear the whole of it. When they were about to begin something else the Prince of Wales said, "No, let us play this over again. I heard M. des Brosses say he would like to hear it all." I willingly relate this trait of politeness and kindness.'

At this time, too, we hear of Charles receiving the present of a full Highland costume from the Duke of Perth, and in acknowledging the gift he says he will wear it with satisfaction for the value and esteem he has for friends like whom he would like to be dressed. The only record of Charles ever having worn the kilt in his early manhood, however, was for one evening at a ball on 8 February 1741, probably just after he had received this gift.

For several years after the death of the 'queen' life in the exiled court had proceeded with little excitement and simple regularity; James was becoming more and more a martyr to his maladies, and melancholy increasingly settled upon him. There is little doubt that he had practically abandoned all hope of personally heading an army of restoration and even of his own restoration at all. He however never relaxed his vigilance and determination to fit his children for their high destiny, should either of them at any time be called to England and the throne of his ancestors.

There was a slight revival of hope at the end of 1738 owing to political differences in England, with the prospect of war breaking out between England and Spain, but little came of it a year later when war was actually declared except for the usual crop of high-spirited and encouraging reports from Scotland that men were ready. However, the cautious and vacillating policy of the English Jacobites, who wrote that it was 'too great a risk' and that nothing could be done without foreign assistance, more than counteracted the enthusiasm of the Scots.

At was at this time that Charles des Brosses was visiting Italy, and his *Letters from Italy* contain other descriptions of 'King James' and his court that are particularly valuable because of the fact that the writer was not in any way or at any time connected with the Chevalier or with Stuart politics. He says that James is

'easily to be recognized for a Stuart, and very like his father and his natural brother, the Duke of Berwick, with the difference that the Duke's countenance was sad and stern, whereas that of the Pretender is sad and feeble. . . . There is no lack of dignity in his manner, and I have never seen any Prince hold a large Court with so much grace and majesty. . . . He speaks little, but always with gentleness and kindness. His table is always laid for eleven persons . . . each time I have been he has asked me to stay. . . . When he comes to table his two sons, before sitting down, kneel and ask his blessing.'

In September 1740, William MacGregor of Balhaldy, who, because of the proscription on the name of his clan, called himself 'Drummond', arrived in Rome with the news that twenty thousand Scotsmen were prepared to rise at once. At the same time, too, the younger Glengarry joined the Jacobite court. He was later to prove to be a traitor in the pay of England.

By 1743 the House of Hanover had become so

much detested in England that George II was denounced by speaker after speaker in the House of Commons as having made England a mere province of Hanover, and everything again seemed ripe for a restoration.

In November James at last agreed to send his son and the Duke of Ormonde to Paris to be in readiness for an invasion of England. In December Balhaldy arrived in Rome with a verbal message from Louis XV to summon the 'Prince of Wales', although it was couched in such uncertain terms that 'James VIII' wrote to the King of France on 23 December:

'I candidly avow to your Majesty that my first impulse was to delay my son's orders and instructions until I could have received more precise orders and instructions; . . . but I finally determined not to constrain my son's ardour to go where his own honour and your Majesty call him.'

On the same day the 'king' signed the prince's commission in the following words:

'Whereas we have a near prospect of being restored to the throne of our ancestors by the good inclination of our subjects towards us and by the assistance of His Most Christian Majesty for that effect, and whereas on account of the present situation of this country it will be absolutely impossible for us to be at the first setting up of our Royal Standard and even for some time after, we therefore esteem it for our service and for the good of our Kingdoms and Dominions to nominate and appoint our dearest son Charles, Prince of Wales, to be sole Regent of our Kingdoms of England, Scotland, and Ireland, and of all other [of] our Dominions during our absence, requiring all our faithful subjects to give all due submission and obedience to our Regent aforesaid, and lastly we dispense with all formalities and other omissions which may be herein contained, declaring this our commission to be as firm and valid as if it had passed our great Seals. Given under our Sign Manual and Privy Seal at our Court at Rome the 23rd day of December, 1743, in the 43rd year of our reign.'

Again, however, the spirit of timidity manifested itself amongst the English Jacobites, and requests were made to defer the expedition until the month of February of the following year. As a consequence the French king countermanded his orders for the fleet at Dunkerque.

Poor 'King James', again distracted at the uncertainty, wrote to Lord Sempill, who was also counselling delay, that it is 'now or never' once again and that Prince Charles shall go to Paris. Prince Charles actually did go on 9 January 1744, never to see his fond father and king again.

By March 1744, all was again lost. Although war between France and Britain was declared, a French spy in British pay had disclosed the plan for an invasion of England, allowing the British Admiralty to activate an effective defence in the English Channel. Count de Saxe, who was to have led the invasion, invaded Flanders instead.

The 'king's' deep and grievous disappointment was intensified by his great anxiety for his son, and he was particularly perturbed at the attitude of the French court, which, although at war with England and responsible for the warlike preparations so recently rendered futile, yet continued to insist upon the prince remaining in hiding and unknown.

Time passed slowly for the anxious father in Rome, who continually pressed the necessity for preserving great caution as to 'wine and play' upon his absent son, and he expressed great concern at the incognito upon which the King of France insisted.

At the end of December 1744, the Chevalier wrote a pathetic letter to Charles in which he described himself as a 'useless old father' who could neither write nor read owing to failing sight.

Three months later a rumour of the proposal to

make a descent upon Scotland without the promised French assistance alarmed James greatly, and he wrote to the prince's entourage not to give any heed to so dangerous a scheme. But the caution born of age and constant disappointment had not yet weakened the gallant spirit of 'Bonnie Prince Charlie', and his reply was to give a full account of his preparations and finances and to advise the Chevalier on 2 July from 'St Lazaire at the mouth of the Loire' that he was embarking that day for Scotland. Advised by exiled Jacobites, Charles had determined that the only way to bring France to his aid was to show that a successful invasion could be made.

Poor, fond, anxious, 'useless old father'! From the very start he made up his mind that the attempt must fail in the absence of foreign assistance, which bitter experience told him would not be forthcoming; yet he did all he possibly could to obtain that help. He wrote urgent letters to the kings of France and Spain, entreating help. He sent his younger son, Henry, to Avignon, to await the French king's instructions, and he even went so far as to write the most pathetic and the most self-effacing letters of all his voluminous correspondence to the king of France and to some of the Jacobite adherents, definitely stating his intention to 'abdicate' in favour of the prince.

31

In his letter to one Jacobite leader he adds the homely and poignant phrase, 'I hope in one fashion or another to be still able to prove to you, and to a few more on this side of the water, that you will have lost nothing by a change of masters,' and again he voices his conviction that if foreign 'troops are not sent to help the Prince his enterprise must fail'.

How right his warning proved to be; it *did* fail. Gloriously and wonderfully near to success as the effort was, it was foredoomed to failure from the very start – as all the Stuart efforts were doomed – but it wrote perhaps the brightest page on Scottish history since Bannockburn, and from that time on it altered the whole outlook of the gallant hearts of those who considered the exiled Stuarts as their rightful kings. From that time on Prince Charlie was the darling of Jacobite hopes and James Francis Edward, the sweet-dispositioned, gallant old Chevalier, gradually subsided into oblivion, a hopeless, failing old man.

On 23 December, Prince Charles received his commission as Regent of the Three Kingdoms, a document that contained the virtual admission from James that he could not himself conduct the campaign for his restoration. The usual delays followed, caused by the inevitable hanging back of the English Jacobite leaders, whom Charles later rightly described as 'affred of their own shaddo', but at last, on 9 January 1744, the prince left Rome with his brother, Henry, under the pretence of going shooting at Cisterna, and with two attendants, Sheridan and O'Sullivan, reached Genoa and finally Antibes, where he was detained for a few days pending orders from Paris to the commandant of the garrison. Released at length, he next travelled via Avignon and Lyons to Paris, where he wrote one of his characteristic misspelt letters to the father he was never to see again, saying that he had 'mett with all that could be expected from King Louis, who expresses great tenderness, and will be careful of my concerns'. Again, a few days later, 'I am in perfect health, and everything gose to a wish. I am very busi in ernest and not in gest as I have been till now, but I do it with great pleasure and attention, it being my duty.'

Then from Paris to Gravelines – where his father had returned with broken spirit and hopes thirty years earlier – and where everything appeared in readiness to embark by 2 March.

The one English adherent who was to have embarked with them to show 'the union amongst the English' actually arrived in Dunkerque but clearly had second thoughts and fled back again without word or message.

Count Maurice of Saxe was in command of the expedition and by 3 March had all his troops on board the transports, the Earl Marischal writing to the Prince of Wales that 'all the troops going to be embarkt are cheerful and hearty' and that the Duke of Ormonde was on his way.

But England, whatever the courage of those of her countrymen who prayed for and drank toasts to the 'King over the Water' in the special glasses that they engraved with the White Rose and 'FIAT' or 'REDEAT' was not served by cowards in her government. Her forces were quickly organized. Even her disaffected soldiers, like Lord Stair, who had left the army in disgust at the king's preference for Hanover, came forward to offer their services.

The eager prince writes to the Earl Marischal that 'the most encouraging accounts possible' are received from the king's friends in England but is sarcastic about the uncertainties of the French orders to the Count de Saxe, which he says 'are shocking'. These order him to proceed to the mouth of the Thames and wait there 'for some of our friends and pilots to come aboard, and if none appear, to return with the troops. . . . Such orders do not sit easy on my stomach, and if it should unhappily happen that neither pilots nor none of them should come aboard to me, I am determined to be with them at whatever rate it is and to live and dye with them.'

Then there was the inevitable storm to damage the Stuart cause. Four days later eleven transports were aground and all the vessels in harbour had lost their small boats. The Count de Saxe wrote to the prince, 'I am in despair at the obscurity and langour reigning over all this affair, desiring nothing more than to give Your Royal Highness proof of the ardour of my zeal to serve him.'

Charles sent an urgent and passionate message to the Earl Marischal asking that the French naval commander of the Isle of Wight should attack Admiral Norris, who was in the Downs, but in reply got the fatal intimation that that could only be done by direct orders from Paris, which would not be given, and that the chiefs of the party, both in England and Scotland, had been arrested or gone into hiding.

The unhappy prince summed up his situation and his fate in his letter to Lord Sempill on 15 March:

'It is my first entry into the world. It will get known that I was near to the place of embarkation, and if I retire without attempting anything after such fine appearances, the whole world will say that the misfortunes of my family are attached to all its generations, and shall never have an end.'

And again to his father, revealing the indomitable spirit that was to carry him so far and yet so fruitlessly:

'You may be persuaded that no disappointment whatsoever will ever discourage me or slacken me in doing what is next best for your service. I have learned from you how to bere with disappointment, and I see it is the only way, which is to submit oneself entirely to the will of God and never to be discouraged.'

And so he waited, eating his heart out in misery and hiding at Gravelines.

A light is thrown on his impetuous character and readiness to accept evidence either for or against his friends in the reception he gave to the Earl Marischal's advice to King Louis not to allow the prince to 'make the campaign' in Flanders with the French king. This was well meant and entirely in the prince's own interest because of the harm it would be likely to do the cause were Charles to appear actually in arms for France against his own countrymen and his father's 'subjects', but the prince chose to see in it as an unwarranted interference in his affairs. He withdrew his confidence from Lord Marischal entirely and unfortunately increased that which he had already placed too much in MacGregor of Balhaldy. The latter's character was not such as would add to the lustre of the prince's own reputation in the eyes of the world.

Louis refused to allow him to take part in the campaign, and on his return to Paris we find the French ministers considerably perturbed at the prince's heavy expenses.

Early in the fateful year '45, the prince seemed to return to the public eye, for he attended the opera, and several functions were arranged in his honour. Still the French did nothing about the promised expedition, and even the British ambassador, Walpole, marvelled at the inactivity and spoke of there being fewer than six thousand troops in the whole of Britain if the attempt were made.

Charles Edward next went to Fitz-James, the pleasant home with which the first Duke of Berwick had provided himself. It was a few miles out of Paris and was placed at the disposal of Prince Charles as a residence by the duke's son, the Bishop of Soissons. Here the prince passed his time rather more pleasantly in field sports while awaiting the call to England, and it was here that he wrote to his father that 'our friends are affred of their own shaddo'.

In March his adherents in Scotland made a move.

The Duke of Hamilton expressed his adherence and offered to advance money for the cause, and Charles was urged to send for Lord Marischal.

The French victory at Fontenoy over the English appeared to create the opportunity so long awaited, and Charles determined to act on his own initiative.

He had borrowed forty thousand livres from his father's banker in Paris, Waters, and he owed another one hundred and twenty thousand to the latter's son, so he wrote an urgent letter to Rome asking the Chevalier's blessing, and that 'all his own jewels', which he had inherited from his mother's father, Prince James Sobieski, 'should be pawned to buy broadswords' and to send money to his Highland adherents, and he expressed himself as determined to go over and 'to dye in the field' rather than remain inactive any longer. He reminded his father that 'you yourself did the like in the year '15' but that circumstances were now more encouraging. He asks his father to come to Avignon 'but take the liberty to advise that you should not ask leave of the French Court'.

In another letter – to James Edgar – he gives an account of his purchases for the campaign and the money he has in hand, and considering that all this had to be done not only without the knowledge of the French court and ministry but that he also kept many of his most intimate friends and personal adherents in the dark, is clear proof of his great ability and force of character now that he was committed to what was to follow.

So, on 2 July 1745, at seven o'clock in the evening, Prince Charles went aboard his little ship *La Doutelle*, and with her escort, the *Elisabeth*, three days later sailed for Scotland from the shores of France and at last set his torch to the heather, no doubt reflecting on the delays that followed the loss of the French transports in 1745 and at the supineness of the English Jacobites who had promised so much and performed so little upon the same occasion.

CHAPTER II

$\mathcal{H}$OUR OF GLORY

Charles had spent a weary year of inactivity between 8 March 1744 and 22 May 1745 in Paris and at Fitz-James until Fontenoy seemed to give him the opportunity he had been waiting for. He immediately became the soul of energy and impatience to make his long-deferred effort.

It had taken the prince a further month of feverish preparation in the purchase of warlike stores and two good ships, aided by, Antoine Walsh and Walter Rutledge – afterwards created an 'earl' and a 'baronet' by 'James VIII' for their services – before the prince boarded *La Doutelle*. They sailed from Nantes on 4 July in high spirits and with hope for the success of his adventure.

His last letter to his father before he sailed contains the commentary that: 'We have nothing to do now but to hope in the Almighty's favouring us, and recompensing our troubles', and shows that as far as he could make them his arrangements for the great venture were complete.

His personal companions were the gallant 'seven men of Moidart', i.e. William Lord Tullibardine, formerly the Duke of Atholl, who was attainted for his share in the '15 rising and his title and estates given to a younger brother, James, who was a supporter of the Hanoverian government, although the elder, of course, was always recognized as the 'Duke' by the Jacobites; Sir John MacDonald, an officer in the Irish Brigade of the French army; Aeneas MacDonald of Kinlochmoidart, the brother of the chieftain of that ilk; Colonel Francis Strickland of Sizergh in Westmorland, whose influence on the prince was a source of anxiety to the Chevalier; Sir Thomas Sheridan, his tutor; Captain William John O'Sullivan, an Irish soldier of fortune and afterwards the prince's quartermaster-general who was to merit Lord George Murray's most contemptuous criticism after Culloden; and the Reverend George Kelly, an Irishman who had formerly been secretary to Bishop Atterbury, a Jacobite cleric, and who must not be confused with the dissolute Father Kelly who was later one of the prince's boon companions in France.

With these others also were a 'Mr Buchanan', of

whom we hear no more that definitely identifies him but who possibly returned with the ship to France; Antoine Walsh, the owner and captain of the vessel; and Michel, the prince's valet.

On 4 July *La Doutelle* was joined at Belleisle by the *Elisabeth*, a French ship of sixty-four guns, fitted out for the prince's purpose by her commander, Walter Rutledge. On 5 July the little expedition set sail for Scotland by way of the west coast of England, and on the 9th sighted an English man-o'-war, the *Lion*. The *Elisabeth* at once engaged the enemy, and the prince on the *Doutelle* entreated her captain to join in the fight. Walsh rightly refused to risk his precious freight and stood on his course, leaving his consort to fight it out. Both the English and French ships were crippled. The *Lion* was forced to draw off, while the *Elisabeth* crept back to Brest, a battered wreck but one that had saved the situation.

On 22 July the prince sighted his promised land, and on the 23rd landed on the subsequently named 'Prince's Strand' (Coilleag a' Phrionnsa) of the little island of Eriskay in the Outer Hebrides.

Full of boyish ardour, the young prince sprang ashore from the galley that had carried him from the ship, and he thrilled with delight and hope at the thought that the king of birds had come to greet the

Prince of Scotland when the Duke of Atholl pointed out to him where a golden eagle hovered in the sky above the *Doutelle*. Duncan Cameron, one of Lochiel's clansmen, gives a clear narrative of the landing and the immediate incidents – they caught some flounders, which were roasted in a hut by the narrator, and Charles laughed heartily at Duncan's cooking.

They spent the night in a shieling belonging to one of Kinlochmoidart's men, Angus MacDonald, and the high-spirited prince amused himself with criticizing the smokiness of the atmosphere of the hut and of the general conditions, which brought down upon him some caustic comments from his host, who appears to have been unaware of his identity.

The party were all naturally in a very excited state, and the records of their movements for some days vary considerably, but Charles sent for the nearest laird, MacDonald of Boisdale, on the following morning and asked for his assistance. Boisdale implored him to 'return home', to which the prince impetuously replied, 'I am come home' and demanded the adherence of the chiefs in the vicinity – MacLeod and MacDonald of Sleat. Both, however, refused, and MacLeod informed the government of the prince's arrival. In this way, at the very outset he was betrayed by some of those on whose loyalty he had been led to believe he could rely.

A few days later the *Doutelle* sailed for Arisaig, and Charles landed at Borradale. Kinlochmoidart joined him at the request of his brother, Aeneas Mac-Donald, and other loyal chiefs began to arrive. With their arrival the prince's spirits continued to soar, and messengers were sent north and east to summon the chiefs to their prince's aid. The letters sent were all similar. Dr Walter Blaikie published one to the Earl of Cromarty in his *Itinerary of Prince Charles Edward Stuart*. This is dated from 'Boradel August the 8th 1745', but another is even more interesting. Written from Borradale and dated 6 August, two days before the letter to the Earl of Cromarty, it runs:

'Being fully perswaded of your loyalty and zeal for the King's service, I think fit to inform you that I am come into this country to assert his right, at the head of such of his faithfull subjects as will engage in his quarrel. I intend therefor to set up the Royale Standard at Glenfinnen on Munday the 19th instant. Your appearance on that occasion would be very usefull, but if not practicable I expect you to joyn me as soon as possible, and you shall always find me ready to give you marks of my friendship.

CHARLES P.R.'

Charles was deaf to all suggestions that he return and await the promised French aid. Even the 'gentle Lochiel' offered this advice but, finding his persuasions futile, at once raised his clan, the Camerons, as also did Clanranald the MacDonalds.

This was enough! Charles was confident of and happy in his success, and it was decided that the standard would be raised on 19 August.

On 1 August, in the meantime, the government had issued a proclamation setting a price of thirty thousand pounds upon the prince's head, and Charles retaliated three weeks later when he heard of it by proclaiming a contemptuous reward of thirty pounds for the capture of the Elector of Hanover. He was afterwards persuaded to alter this insulting sum to a similar amount to that offered for his own arrest, which he did in a dignified document that protested against 'a practice so unusual amongst Christian Princes' and placing the blame upon those who had 'set such an infamous example'.

On 4 August the *Doutelle* left, and on 11 August the prince, now with a bodyguard of MacDonalds and with a train of artillery, went to Kinlochmoidart House.

Meanwhile Lord President Forbes, for the government, had raised a full regiment of Highlanders under the command of Lord Loudoun to oppose the rapidly growing Jacobite army.

The fiery cross was sent around by the Jacobite supporters, however, and in this way the clans were warned that all those who did not join the prince would have their cottages burned and their cattle maimed by the royalist clans.

Ewan MacPherson of Cluny, afterwards the prince's very loyal adherent, was at that time an officer in King George's army, so the MacPhersons held aloof in Badenoch and even sent an urgent message to General Cope to march north and stem the tide of invasion, while the Hanoverian Duke of Atholl, 'James the Whig', sent his younger brother, Lord George Murray – also afterwards a renowned Jacobite commander and the best soldier in the prince's service – to act with Cope.

The first shots were fired at Spean Bridge, where an action was fought by MacDonald of Tiendrish and resulted in the capture of two companies of the Royal Scots on their way to strengthen the garrison at Fort William.

These early successes delighted the young prince, who was now, by his father's commission, Prince Regent of Scotland and England, and it was with high hopes and spirits that he marched to Loch Shiel and travelled by boat to Glenaladale, where he spent the night before the raising of the royal standard.

On 19 August, early in the morning, he went by boat to Glenfinnan, at the far end of the loch, and with a bodyguard of fifty of Clanranald's men the royal ensign was floated on the breeze by the Duke of Atholl in a gathering of six hundred of the MacDonalds under Clanranald and about the same number of Camerons under Lochiel. The prince made a spirited speech, and the Highlanders responded by tossing their bonnets into the air to the sound of the 'gathering' played by the pipers of the two clans.

Sending their baggage forward to Loch Lochy, the prince stayed at Kinlochiel, from where he sent a message to Grant of Grant and Stewart of Appin to join him. He received no reply from the former chieftain but Stewart joined the standard with six hundred men four days later.

At Kinlochiel, too, the prince learned that General Cope was marching to meet him by Dalwhinnie. At Moy he appointed John Murray of Broughton as his secretary and then proceeded to Invergarry Castle, where he was met by Fraser of Gortleg with a message begging him to march north to Inverness and assuring him that he would then be joined by the

Frasers, MacKenzies, MacLeods, Grants and Mack-
intoshes. The Grants of Glen Moriston came in, and
the MacDonalds of Glen Garry and Glencoe, but the
Jacobite Duke of Atholl pressed the prince to march
south and raise the Atholl men, with whose assistance they could make themselves masters of Edinburgh.

This plan appealed to the adventurous prince and
was put into action at once. The wild Corrieyairack
Pass, the highest point on General Wade's Highland
road (which had been made thirty years before for
subduing the Highlands), was crossed, but the elated
army found that General Cope had marched north
to avoid a meeting and was heading for Inverness instead of awaiting his enemy, as expected, on the level
ground at the foot of the Pass and so disputing the
road to Blair Atholl and the south. So Charles and his
little army swept on.

The prince now obtained one of his greatest adherents in Ewan MacPherson the younger of Cluny,
whom he had taken prisoner in his own Cluny Castle on the banks of the Spey. There is little doubt that
Cluny was a 'willing prisoner' and that his capture
was more or less a 'blind'.

Duncan Forbes of Culloden had written him a letter with a view to preventing Cluny joining the

prince. Only a month or two before he had been approached by all his brother chieftains to protect the country from thieves and robbers who were harrying the cattle, and for his services with 'Cluny's Watch' (a forerunner of the 'Black Watch' or 42nd Regiment of Highlanders) had been given a company in Lord Loudoun's Regiment of Highlanders enrolled for the same purpose, but neither this fact nor Lord President Forbes's letter, nor the defection of MacLeod and MacDonald made known to him in it, could prevent Cluny MacPherson from joining his rightful prince.

The Lord President's letter reads as follows:

'DEAR SIR, – I received yours of the 19th this evening – But about 2 hours before your messenger came, I had dispatched an express to John MacPherson, with a letter to you, which I hope will come safe to hand, But lest it should loiter by the way I enclose a copy of it; The advice I there give is my sincere opinion – paper bullots such as the printed declaration (for the transmitting of which I thank you,) do generally but small execution, & I should hope Prudence, as well as Humanity, will prevent unnecessary severitys, which can lead only with men of Resolution to exasperatn. Should steadyness to their Duty bring any country under hardships, I trust, as in my former letter I have

mentioned, that an indemnification process will en-
sue – your letter to the Generall (wherof you sent me
the copy), is exceeding right, and there is only one
thing which I wish you had not expressed so strong,
and that is when you say that *most of all the Highland
chieftains* – are with the Young Invader, for contrary to
what you have been informed of concerning Sir
Allexdrs. MacDonald and MacLeod; I do assure you
that they are both, in the same disposition that you
and I are, that they have absolutely refused to join,
and have prevented the stirring of Garry men of their
dependence, and my authority for saying so is no less
than letters under the hands of both, the last of which
I received, this day about 5 a clock; it is dated the
17th Sept. 2 a clock afternoon, and written by Mac-
Leod, in answer to one that I had sent him by express
from this plase after my arrivall – I mention this to
you for your private satisfaction, that you may not be
imposed on, by reports, which will be purposely
raised, to intimidate some & delude others; but I
would not have their correspondence with me spo-
ken of but to friends, Because it is unnecessary, it
should not be publick – if they had any expectations
of your friend Lovat, they are vastly mistaken, and
Seafort acquaints me he has orderd a rendezvous of
his people. The letter which in mine of this afternoons date, I desired you to send forward to the Generall, under the Duke of Atholls cover says so much of

the prospects of his speedy marching, that I need not write to him over again; I desire to hear from you as often as anything occurs – the bearer must sleep here as the night is very dark, and is to start in the morning to get at you.

'I am, dear sir, very faithfully yours,

DUN. FORBES.'

'CULLODEN, Tuesday 20th August, 8 at night.'

Cope, hurrying north by the Spey, hoped to raise the Grants for the government but found the young son of the chieftain, Ludovic Grant, inclined to 'sit on the fence' under the plea of the necessity to defend Castle Grant and to create a diversion in the event of a pursuit by the superior Highland army, so the clan remained on Speyside.

At Dalwhinnie Cluny had been brought to the prince and himself admits that after the insulting treatment he had received from Cope 'an angel could not resist the soothing close applications' of his captor. He was, however, kept a 'prisoner' until the army reached Perth a week later. There he was released and returned through Glen Garry and over the Drumochter Pass to Badenoch to raise his clan for the prince. This was indeed a hazardous undertaking, and Cluny's venture must arouse the admiration of everyone who considers it. He had to retrace his steps alone over some seventy miles of the wildest mountain country, in the rear of the rebel forces, towards that English army in which he had been serving only a week before and from which he was now a deserter. Were he captured his fate would have been certain and immediate.

We have no record of his journey or of his movements while Cope was marching on to the north of him to Elgin and Aberdeen, nor have we evidence of any negotiations with his neighbouring chieftain, Grant of Grant, but Cluny's influence was strong enough to hold both at bay while his clan was being raised and armed, and for six weeks of feverish activity Cluny maintained his hold on Badenoch until he rejoined his prince in Edinburgh on 29 October, to be followed by the MacPhersons, four hundred strong, two days later.

Cluny's action in hurrying south to Edinburgh in advance of the clan was undoubtedly the result of receiving a letter from the prince's secretary, John Murray of Broughton. It is dated 'Edinburgh, Oct. the 24th 1745' and reads:

'To Coll McPherson of Cluny.
'Sir, – It's now a long time since you have been expected to join the Army either with or without the

Duke of Atholl but to our great surprise we are informed you returned to the country to bring up more men. The 300 we were told are with you are now of more use than double their number can be some time hence for which reason the prince has ordered me to write you by express to march up with all dilligence to join him without waiting for the Duke. Should he make any further delay which at the same time there is no reason to believe as the Prince has sent him express orders to march immediately from Perth I must again repeat to you that upon receipt of this you may not delay an half hour and make as long marches as possible. There are arms in plenty at Perth and Dunkeld of which I suppose you have already had your share.

'I am with the utmost impatience to see you your most obedt and most humble serv^t

J^{NO} MURRAY.'

Blank commissions, sealed with the royal arms of England as borne by James II and signed by the prince, are still in existence. Some are for the appointment of lieutenants and others of captains, and from the date that they all bear they are evidently some of a number of similar forms issued by the prince to the chief of the MacPhersons before his departure from Perth to raise his clan and form it into a regiment. The wording, except for the rank of the recipient, is identical in all cases and is similar to the commission made out in the name of Ewan MacPherson of Cluny himself, which runs as follows:

'CHARLES PRINCE OF WALES &C., REGENT OF SCOTLAND ENGLAND FRANCE AND IRELAND AND THE DOMINIONS THEREUNTO BELONGING.

'To our trusty and well-beloved Evan Macpherson of Cluny, greeting.

'We reposing especiall trust and confidence in your courage, loyalty and good conduct do hereby constitute and appoint you to be a Collonell in his Majesties Forces and to take your rank in the Army as such from the date hereof. You are therefore carefully and diligently to discharge the duty and trust of Collonell aforesaid by doing and performing everything which belongs thereto. And we hereby require all and every the officers and soldiers to observe and obey you as a Collonell and yourself to observe and follow all such orders and directions as you shall from time to time receive from us our Commander in chief for the time being or any other your Superior Officer according to the Rules and Discipline of War in pursuance of the trust hereby reposed in you.

'Given at Perth this Seventh September 1745.

CHARLES P.R.'

The name in each other case is left blank, to be filled in by the clan chieftain.

Meanwhile 'Charles the adventurer' had become a prince indeed, at the head of a gallant and enthusiastic army. His brave spirit and his kindliness won him friends in every town through which he passed. In Perth he was joined by the Duke of Perth and Lord George Murray, who were appointed generals of his army, and by James Johnstone, the son of an Edinburgh merchant who later served in the French army in America, earning him the title of Chevalier de Johnstone. Charles's father's proclamation as 'King James VIII' and his own as 'Prince Regent of the Kingdom' were read in Perth and in Dundee.

The clans were hastening to join his colours. Robertsons (two hundred), MacGregors (one hundred and fifty), Grants of Glen Moriston (one hundred), MacLachlans (one hundred and fifty) and some local gentry and their servants, with his previous forces, made up an army of about two thousand five hundred by the time that the first battle of the campaign – Prestonpans or Gladsmuir – was fought on 21 September.

Of the prince himself at this time, there are several anecdotes. Even the Whig factor left behind by the Hanoverian Duke of Atholl at Blair Castle calls him 'good natured', although he thinks that he 'hath not very much in him' and describes the Highland army as 'the poorest naked creatures and ill armed'.

At Lude House he joined in the Highland dances and called for the old song 'This is no' my ain hoose' to be played.

At Dunkeld Charles spoke tenderly of his young brother, the Duke of York, as 'much to be pitied' and stated that 'few brothers love as we do'.

Maxwell of Kirkconnell states (in his *Narrative of Charles Prince of Wales's Expedition to Scotland*) that the dissensions between Charles and Lord George Murray, his most able general, began almost immediately and were fostered by John Murray of Broughton, who 'assured the Prince that Lord George had joined him on purpose to have an opportunity of delivering him up to the Government'. Charles unfortunately listened to the slander and showed that fatal tendency to believe any tale, either good or evil, that was whispered in his ear by his unscrupulous secretary, and undoubtedly Lord George himself contributed to the jealous insinuations of his unworthy rival by 'such violent sallies as the Prince could not digest'.

These dissensions were to continue with increasing violence throughout the whole of the campaign and went a long way towards being a main cause of its undoing. Charles never really trusted Lord George, and although that gallant soldier lost everything he had in his service, the prince treated him with studied disdain in his subsequent relations with him in France.

On 11 September Charles visited the Palace of Scone, where his father had stayed and had been crowned in 1715, and was at last in the home of his ancestors. From there he marched to Dunblane, where he won many hearts by his gracious manner. At Doune he crossed the River Forth at the Fords of Frew, where an Edinburgh contemporary news-sheet (*The Caledonian Mercury*, 1745) states that 'the young Chevalier had been the first who put foot in the water, and waded through the Forth at the head of his detachment'. As he approached this important ford, which Colonel Gardiner's dragoons had been specially sent to guard, the English cavalry retired to Linlithgow.

The frowning castle of Stirling came into view of the little army, and its guns were trained upon them and fired but apparently did no damage.

Charles dined with Sir Hugh Patterson at Bannockburn House, where he was fated to meet his *belle amie*, Clementina Walkinshaw, on his return march in the following spring. He reached Falkirk on 14 September, and the following morning took possession of the Palace of Linlithgow, the birthplace of Mary Queen of Scots.

Edinburgh was now directly in front of the bloodless army, and from Corstorphine the prince sent a message to the magistrates demanding the surrender of the city. They replied by asking for time to consider, which was refused them, and on the night of 16 September a body of nine hundred men under Lochiel marched to the Netherbow Port and arrived just as the gate was opened to admit the returning magisterial deputation. To gain access and march in at the head of his Camerons was an easy task for Lochiel, and he found himself master of the city without striking a blow.

The prince, avoiding the castle's guns, marched to Holyrood and there took up his residence. Heralds and pursuivants were secured, and in robes of office proclaimed James VIII as king of Scotland and Charles as prince regent at the ancient Mercat Cross of Edinburgh.

The playwright and historian John Home describes the prince in his *History of the Rebellion in the Year 1745* as 'tall and handsome, of a fair complexion: he had a light-coloured periwig with his own hair combed over the front. He wore the Highland dress, that is a tartan short coat without the plaid, a blue bonnet on his head, and on his breast the Star of the Order of St Andrew.' The Duke of Perth rode on his right, Lord Elcho on his left, and he 'seemed very thoughtful'.

Charles showed himself and bowed to the crowds from the open window at Holyrood. Mrs Murray, wife of his secretary, sat on horseback outside the gates, with a drawn sword in her hand, distributing white cockades.

On 18 September the army was in camp at Duddingston. Cope's army landed at Dunbar and, reinforced by Gardiner's oft-fleeing dragoons, marched to Haddington and reached Prestonpans on 20 September. Eager to engage them in battle, Charles had left Holyrood, joined his army at Duddingston and marched by Musselburgh to Prestonpans, where he 'slept on the field, lying on the ground without any covering but his plaid'.

The armies were very equal in numbers: Sir John Cope's is given as two thousand five hundred and sixty, and the prince's as two thousand five hundred and eighty. A contemporary account in the *Caledonian Mercury* states that the prince made a speech before the army moved off, which he concluded with the words, 'Gentlemen, I have flung away the scabbard, and with God's assistance I don't doubt of making you a free and happy people.'

In less than a quarter of an hour, early on the morning of 21 September, the battle was over, the remnants of Cope's army in flight except for those who were wounded, killed or taken prisoner. Colonel Gardiner was killed by the Camerons' claymores and Lochaber axes, and the cavalry 'ran like rabets' – as Charles wrote to his father. He showed that humanity after the battle that distinguished his entire campaign and makes a powerful contrast to that of the Duke of Cumberland after Culloden. James Maxwell of Kirkconnell says in his *Narrative of Charles Prince of Wales's Expedition to Scotland* that the slaughter was soon stopped by the prince and the gentlemen of his army, 'who all exerted themselves on this occasion, and got even more honour by their humanity than by their bravery', and many other contemporary accounts pay similar tribute to the prince's humane conduct.

Many of Cope's Highlanders joined the prince's army after the battle, and a council of war was held to discuss the question of marching at once to Berwick and into England, but it was rightly considered that the army was not strong enough to keep open long lines of communication and a return to Edinburgh was decided upon to give the prince's friends time to rise and join him.

On 22 September Charles returned to Holyrood and for nearly five weeks held a court there that rivalled any that had been held within its ancient walls in terms of glory and brilliance.

Every morning the prince regent held a levee of his officers and the citizens. Each morning, too, a strong council assembled to discuss plans, and when that broke up the prince dined in public, attended by his personal staff and the Highland chiefs. In the afternoons he attended the camp and reviewed the various clans, and in the evenings received groups of the ladies of Edinburgh who attended his drawing rooms. He was thronged by a 'vast affluence of well-dressed people', says Maxwell of Kirkconnell. 'Everybody was taken with the prince's figure and general behaviour.' His attire was rich in the extreme, and he frequently wore his Highland garb at his reviews and in the evenings.

The scene in the long gallery at Holyrood – where he 'touched for the evil' on one occasion – must have been extremely brilliant as the handsome young prince, attended by a glittering staff of Highland chieftains and officers, advanced through lanes of curtseying beauties to his public banquets. At other times Charles held his levees in the varied court costumes of France and Italy, which he had brought with him for such occasions, but generally, and always when on the march, his garb was the doublet and kilt of Royal Stuart tartan, with the broad light-blue ribband and the Star of the Garter or of St Andrew on his breast.

Not a breath of scandal was ever breathed against the central figure of the rebellion throughout his stay in Scotland. Indeed, the reproach was that he was 'too chaste'. He showed little liking for feminine society, and except that he is said to have kissed the pretty daughter of Anderson of Windygoul, who brought him a cup of wine on his march to Prestonpans and whose brother led the Highland army across the morass of Gladsmuir to attack Cope, it is rare that a woman's name is even mentioned in connection with that of Charles Edward during his stay in Edinburgh.

The weeks slipped by without much happening of note. The castle held out against the prince, and he attempted to reduce it by stopping supplies. Its commander, General Guest, retaliated by a letter to the magistrates, threatening a bombardment if the prince's orders were obeyed. He actually did fire upon the town and did some damage, as a result of which, in the interests of humanity, a proclamation was issued by the prince permitting communication with the castle to be resumed under special passes. This was published in the *Caledonian Mercury* of 2 October 1745.

The clans were still coming in, and the numbers of the army were swelling until, as the end of October approached, they numbered close to five thousand.

Meanwhile, in Edinburgh, working quietly at his profession as an engraver and lodging in Stewart's Close, was a young man from Orkney of considerable artistic promise, Robert Strange, who was engaged to Isabella Lumisden, sister of one of the prince's adherents, Andrew Lumisden, who afterwards became his secretary after serving the Chevalier for many years in a similar capacity.

Isabella, like so many of the beauties of Edinburgh, was wholeheartedly and enthusiastically engaged in obtaining recruits for the Jacobite army, and as was narrated (in *Memoirs of Sir Robert Strange*), she made it a condition with her lover, betrothed to her at the time as he was, that he should fight for her prince. Robert Strange therefore joined the army as one of the Corps of Royal Life Guards and subsequently accompanied it in all its actions, but in the six weeks of its stay in Edinburgh he was not idle at his legitimate trade, and he was commissioned, doubtless at the instigation of the fair Isabella, to engrave a half-length portrait of the prince in which Charles looks out of an oval window, or frame, over a stone ledge, or pedestal. This portrait was the first known work of Sir Robert Strange and 'was regarded as a wonder of art by those visitors of distinction who watched its progress with the interest of partisans'. Robert Strange painted a few miniature versions of this portrait when living in Paris between 1748 and 1750 as a means of livelihood in exile.

Towards the end of the month news arrived from France that an expedition with six thousand men was ready at Dunkerque, and a treaty was entered into at Fontainebleu under which the King of France undertook to aid the prince 'as far as practicable', but this really bound Louis XV to nothing.

On 30 October a fateful council meeting discussed the question of the march into England. The prince wished to attack General Wade at once and to march on Newcastle-upon-Tyne for that purpose, Wade having only just arrived there with tired troops. Lord George Murray, on the other hand, desired to avoid a battle until either the French assistance arrived or a material increase in their numbers was provided by the English adherents whom they expected to flock to the prince's standard, particularly the Jacobites of Lancashire and Cheshire who would join them on that route. No decision was reached that day, but on the following day Charles, while still holding to his own opinion that an immediate meeting with Wade was preferable, agreed to the Carlisle route. It was decided to divide the small army into two sections, one to march to Kelso and by Liddesdale to Carlisle as a feint of appearing to threaten General Wade at Newcastle, and the other direct to Carlisle by Peebles and Lockerbie.

That night the prince slept at Pinkie House, his time of splendour at Holyrood over.

CHAPTER III

$\mathcal{I}$NVASION OF ENGLAND

On 15 October Charles had written to the Chevalier that 'having with me near eight thousand men and three hundred hors at lest', he was about to essay his epic attempt, and although Andrew Lang seems to accept these figures, the estimate would appear to be somewhat exaggerated, and it is probable that the entire force did not exceed five thousand, as stated in the various records of the clans and units that composed the army.

The prince's personal character on the march stands the acid test of his most inveterate critic at a later date, Lord Elcho, who, according to the same authority, stated that:

'his body was made for war, and he did not spare it, usually sleeping in his boots. He marched at the head of the clans; people thought that it was only for a mile or two to encourage the soldiers at the beginning, and were surprised to see him continue all day, but it was the same every day after, during the whole expedition. In dirty lanes and deep snow he took his chance with the common men, and would seldom be prevailed upon to get on horseback to cross a river. It's not to be imagined how much this manner of bringing himself down to a level with the men and his affable behaviour with the meanest of them endeared him to the army. He came to Lauder, when hearing that some of the Highlanders lagged behind, with a view, as was thought, of deserting, he got on horseback before it was light, went two or three miles back, and brought most of the stragglers up with him.'

In corroboration of Lord Elcho's description of the prince, the following remarkably similar account can be quoted, written by an officer of volunteers in the Duke of Cumberland's army – Ray of Whitehaven – who served throughout the entire campaign after the capture of Carlisle to the final rout at Culloden, where he exults in the slaughter of 'over 2000 Highlandmen' at and directly after the battle. Mr Ray is not only antagonistic but contemptuous of the Jacobites throughout, and, as in the last paragraph of his *History of the Rebellion in 1745* (privately

67

printed in 1755), often inaccurate, but this only makes the tribute that he pays to Charles himself in this case the more valuable:

'His dress was a Highland garb of fine silk tartan, red velvet breeches, and a blue velvet bonnet, with gold lace round it; on his breast a large jewel with St Andrew appended; is about six feet high; walks well and streight, and speaks both *English* and broad *Scotch* very well. For a while he affected to imitate the example of *Charles* XII of Sweden, marching all the day on foot, and every river they were to cross, he was the first man that leap'd into it; he din'd with his soldiers in the open field, and slept on the ground, wrapped in his plaid; at this time the weather was warm. This course of life he follow'd for some time, but his *Italian* constitution not being enur'd to such kind of hardship, after his arrival at Edinburgh, he indulg'd himself in all the conveniences he could procure for his ease and pleasure.'

On 1 November 1745, the gallant little army began the most romantic and desperate invasion that England had ever known. Fired with loyalty and enthusiasm, and elated by their easy victory over Sir John Cope, five thousand Highlanders and five hundred cavalry set out to conquer the armies of England and Hanover and to win a throne for the man they regarded as their rightful king.

Charles dispatched a small body of horse to make a diversion towards Wooler in order to create the impression that he was advancing on Newcastle, but he himself marched at the head of his clans towards Carlisle, where he joined the Jacobite Duke of Atholl's column on 9 November, crossed the River Eden and set up camp on the west side of the town. On the following day he summoned the garrison to surrender and encamped his army at Brampton in order to intercept and engage General Wade in the event of his attempting to relieve Carlisle. On 15 November the castle and town surrendered, and with that magnanimity that characterized his conduct throughout the entire campaign, he dismissed the garrison to their homes.

At this juncture Lord George Murray took offence at the fact that the Duke of Perth had been instructed to arrange terms for the surrender of the castle and resigned his commission as lieutenant-general. This, however, the officers would not accept, and upon his resuming, the Duke of Perth in turn resigned his in favour of Murray and thereafter served as a regimental commander under him.

It is obvious that Lord George Murray at this period, undoubted as were his military qualifications, created the first differences that were eventually to have such harmful effects upon the council. His services were invaluable, and it cannot be denied that without them events could not have prospered as much as they did, but on the other hand his obstinate jealousy and his hasty impatience with his prince in such a venture were inexcusable.

On 17 November the prince and his troops entered Carlisle and remained there until 20 November, and during this occupancy a further council was held to decide on future movements. One section of the chiefs was anxious to remain at Carlisle to see if the English Jacobites would rise, but a larger body of opinion was in favour of marching through Lancashire towards London in order to remove all possible pretext from the English Jacobites for neglecting to join the rebels.

Through the whole length of the stay in what was then Cumberland only two recruits joined the army, and although, as Andrew Lang says, the prince was welcomed at Warwick House on the Eden by a daughter of the Howards of Corby and that 'in Corby a set of portraits of the exiled Stuarts exists, as others do from Esk to Exe in Jacobite houses, from which not a man nor a guinea was sent to help the cause,' his consternation at the early evidence that the English Jacobites were still 'affred of their own shaddo' was apparent to all his personal staff.

The discipline of the army was very severe. Lochiel ordered one of his Camerons to be shot for thieving, and one of the Monroes also was executed, while all requisitions were most scrupulously paid for, and it is stated that Charles made a practice of leaving a handsome tip for the servants in houses where he took up his personal quarters.

The army marched to Penrith and then on to Kendal after a day's halt. On 24 November an English sloop of war, the *Hazard*, was captured by stratagem at Montrose and pressed into the prince's service. Steadily the army marched on, through Lancaster to Preston where the prince was joined by his one recruit of importance, Francis Townley, as well as by William Vaughan. A few others from North Wales joined his standard, but the considerable levies that were expected from the English Jacobites did not materialize, either at Preston or at Manchester, which latter town was reached on 29 November. The total of the Manchester recruits did not exceed three hundred men, whereas several thousands had been looked for, and by degrees it was borne in upon the leaders that they were advancing into the country of an enemy with a force at least twice that of their own size in front of them and with Wade's army of their own size on their flank and rear, so that the march must end in disaster.

The little body of recruits was formed into the Manchester Regiment and placed under the command of Francis Townley. The town was illuminated and bonfires lit in all directions, and it was still hoped that the activities of the Welsh Jacobites under Sir Watkin Williams Wynn and other prominent members of the Cycle Club would result in further large enrolments, but these good gentlemen, ready as they were to drink toasts to the 'king' and the prince in their specially engraved glasses, made no move until it was too late, and by the time they were ready the retreat had begun and their courage rapidly evaporated.

At Manchester Lord George Murray himself proposed the extension of the march to Derby, in spite of the fact that some of his supporters were already talking of a retreat in the absence of the expected reinforcements.

The prince's appearance at the head of his troops in Manchester can be definitely recorded here:

'Prince Charles entered Manchester at 2 o'clock in

the afternoon, walking in the midst of a select body of the Clans. His dress was a light tartan plaid, belted with a blue sash, and he wore a grey wig over his own fair hair, and the blue velvet bonnet which seems to have been his covering throughout the whole campaign was now adorned in the centre of the top with a white rose to distinguish him from his officers, all of whom wore their cockades on one side.'

Through the fair Staffordshire and Derbyshire lanes to Congleton and Ashbourne Lord George Murray led his column and forced the advance guard of the Duke of Cumberland to retire from Newcastle-under-Lyme to Stone. Meanwhile the prince, with the main body, marched from Macclesfield to Leek, from there to Ashbourne and Derby, the extreme southernmost point of the route being at the crossing over the Trent at Swarkstone Bridge, which was reached on 4 December.

At this time Wade was at Wetherby and the Duke of Cumberland at Lichfield, while a third army was being rapidly formed at Finchley to resist any attempt on London, and on the day following the arrival of the prince at Derby, where he was received by cheering crowds wearing white rosettes but found no one with sufficient courage to join him, that fatal council was held which eventually decided upon the retreat.

The prince begged, in great distress, to proceed at all costs, but he was alone in the wish, not a single member of the council supporting him, as indeed they could scarcely be expected to do in such a hopeless position. He was compelled, therefore, to agree, and Lord George Murray was appointed to command the rearguard in the retreat.

Lang says that 'the army were in the highest spirits, and were taking the Sacrament and sharpening their swords in crowds before the shops of the cutlers,' and also that the Duke of Newcastle was pondering which side he would take and that there was a run on the bank in London, but it is obvious that the numbers of the Jacobite army were greatly exaggerated, so that although the English generals and ministers were in a thorough panic, it was hopeless to expect that army to withstand the forces already assembled against it. To a military mind such as that of Lord George Murray the fact that with little more than five thousand men he had to face some thirty thousand is sufficient to absolve him from any dereliction of duty in refusing to proceed farther, even at his prince's urging.

It is quite certain that Charles's indomitable spirit, his high courage and his enthusiasm had never failed him up to this point in spite of the disappointments that he had endured at Carlisle and Manchester in the lack of recruits, but from the morning of 'Black Friday', 6 December, his whole aspect changed. He became abstracted and melancholy, his 'sweet nature', as one chronicler describes it, becoming morose and passionate, and on many occasions he gave way to displays of temper. According to Lang 'the council left him a sullen and embittered man, and the iron entered into his soul.' Can we wonder that the bitterness of his disappointment and the cruelty of his fate should have turned the high-souled and gracious youth into the debauched misanthrope that he eventually became?

We need not dwell at any length upon the retreat, which took exactly the same road as far as Carlisle as the advance had done, and the Border town was reached on 19 December. On the way the Duke of Perth had a skirmish on the Shap Pass, and on 17 December Cumberland's advance overtook Lord George Murray's rearguard at Clifton, where an action was fought close to Lowther Castle.

Cluny MacPherson appears to have been the officer chiefly involved. A man who was observed to rush from Lord Lowther's house was captured, and from him it was learnt that he was the Duke of Cumberland's 'running footman' and had been sent to intimate that the duke would sleep at Lowther on the pursuit. Cluny was in command of a part of Lord George's rearguard, composed of roughly about three hundred MacPhersons, and he organized a clever ambush of the English cavalry upon whom the Highlanders charged with their old impetuous ardour. The accounts of this skirmish have been much confused, and Andrew Lang gives all the credit of the action to Lord George Murray, while the Chevalier Johnstone attributes to Lochiel the part played by Cluny, but 'evidently by mistake', as Dr Blaikie says, and this is corroborated by existing papers.

Perhaps the most interesting of these is a document, unfortunately unsigned but in the writing of Ewan Macpherson of the '45, which gives a clear account of this action. This reads as follows:

'The Duke of Cumberland (as they call him) came up to us at Clifton very late Wednesday last the eighteenth accompanied with 4000 horse or rather better than three, according to our information, and 2000 foot about a day or two's march behind him. He indeed surprized us as we had no right intelligence about him, and when he appeared there happened to be no more of our Army at hand than Glengaries, Stewart of Apin and my regiments. The rest of the

Armie being at such distance that they could not assist us at the time, our three regiments planted themselves to receive the enemy being commanded by our Generall Lord George Murray. Glengaries regimt were planted at the back of a stone dyke on our right, the Apin regimt in the centre, and mine on the left lineing a hedge wherefrom we expected to attack the enemie on there march towards us. But the generall spying another hedge about a gunshot nearer to the grand army of the enemie which he thought to be more advantageous, ordered my regimt and the Stewarts to possess themselves of that hedge. Directly and at the same time planted himself at the right of my regimt which put me to the left. Immediately we made towards the last mentioned hedge without any cover, which hedge was without our knowing of it lined by the enemie and was so very closs having a deep ditch, that it was much the same as if they had been intrenchd to the teeth. Upon advancing towards them we received a most warm fire, I mean my regimt single wch we soon returned and upon discharging all our firelocks attacked them sword in hand, beat them out of their intrenchmts and put them all to the flight, in a word the whole ditch the enemie had lined, was all filled up with their dead bodies so that we had no difficulty in crossing it. This was only one advanced body of about six hundred dragoons that had dismounted, in order as we think to try if we durst face them. But I suppose they were so well peppered that they will not be hasty in attacking us again. Glengaries regimt fired very briskly from the back of the stone dyke on the right, on a part of the enemy that marchd directly to have flankd us which routed that party; for ought I think they did not lose above a man or two. The Stewarts did not attack in a bodie, a few of them by accident came in our rier by which means they did not lose a man. I had twelve men and a sergt killed on the spot and three privat men wounded but not one officer eyr killed or wounded. We cannot be positive how many were killed of the enemie but that it is generally said by the country men that they were a hundred and fifty and a great many wounded . . . we have great reason to thank all mighty God for our coming so safe off as the attack being after nightfall was one of the most desperate ones have been heard of for a long time, which is allowed by all the officers here as well Scots as French who say that the part my regt played was one of the most gallant things happened in this age and say it was ane action worthy to be recorded if done by the oldest and best disciplined regimt in Europe. Upon beating of all back that had advanced to the main body of the enemy we retyred and charged again to be readie for a second attack at which time we received express orders from the prince to return to Penrith.'

This should finally remove any confusion or doubt as to the facts of the engagement at Clifton.

On the following day they entered Carlisle, where dispatches reached the prince with encouraging accounts of the army assembled in Perth by Lord Strathallen and Lord John Drummond to wait until the French assistance arrived, and at a council of war subsequently held it was decided to march to Perth to link up with this fresh army and to leave a garrison in Carlisle to impede the Duke of Cumberland's advance. The prince has been bitterly criticized, even by his own friends, for leaving this garrison to its fate, but it must not be overlooked that he never abandoned his hope of the conquest of England – he only required reinforcements to put that hope into practice – and even in the latest skirmish at Clifton his troops had shown how easy it was, with their impetuosity, to keep control of the situation. Cumberland claimed this as a victory, but the fact remains that he made no further attempt to press closely on the rear of the retreating army, and Carlisle was a strongly fortified town, so that the task of the garrison, although leaving it must undoubtedly be considered a mistake, did not then appear so hopeless as it seems to have been in the light of later events. In the event, Townley and his gallant defenders had to surrender at discretion to Cumberland's superior forces. They were thereafter treated with the utmost severity, and half the officers, including Townley, and many of the rank and file were executed by the bloodthirsty English commander.

Leaving his garrison and much of his ordnance behind in Carlisle, the prince's army crossed the Esk on his twenty-fifth birthday. Lord George Murray, with a considerable detachment, meanwhile took the original route and arrived in Glasgow a day in advance of the main army commanded by the prince, whose route was materially different from that by which he had entered England. By Dumfries and Drumlanrig Castle he crossed Nithsdale, and by the Menock Pass reached Douglas Castle, where the army bivouacked on the 23rd and where the prince is traditionally stated to have been 'taciturn and gloomy, scarce speaking a word'.

At Hamilton on the following day, however, Dr Blaikie states that he spent a day hunting. On the 26th he entered Glasgow on foot, at the head of his clans as usual, in his war-stained tartan and with his targe, or shield, upon his shoulder. This was the famous targe with silver bosses and ornamentation of the Medusa head that was kept in the hall at Cluny Castle, with many other personal relics of the ill-fated prince and of Cluny's ancestor of 1745, until the collection was dispersed in the early twentieth century.

Charles had ordered the army at Perth under Lords Strathallen and John Drummond to march to join him and enable him to relieve Carlisle, but an inexplicable delay occurred, and the garrison was lost, the Perth army linking up with him only after his arrival in Glasgow.

In Glasgow the prince, saddened and disheartened as he was, kept up the semblance of a court and reviewed his entire army on Glasgow Green. Dr Blaikie, quoting from Maxwell of Kirkconnell's *Narrative of Charles Prince of Wales's Expedition to Scotland*, says:

'It was the first general review he had made since he had left the Highlands. Hitherto he had carefully concealed his weakness, but now, thinking himself sure of doubling his army in a few days, he was not unwilling to let the world see with what a handful of men he had penetrated so far into England and retired almost without any loss. It was indeed a very extraordinary expedition, whether we consider the boldness in the undertaking or the conduct in the execution.'

We may well endorse this view. The total loss by desertion or casualty during the period that elapsed between the crossing of the Esk near Riddings on the advance and its recrossing on the retreat was fewer than forty men.

While in Glasgow the news of the surrender of the Carlisle garrison reached the prince and added to his dejection and melancholy, now commented upon by many contemporary observers. The situation as regards the force of the gradually increasing and enveloping enemy was becoming desperate and needed a desperate remedy. Ever ready for an audacious move Charles provided this in a decision to attempt the capture of Stirling and the frowning fortilace of its castle, and on 3 January 1746 this project was attempted and very nearly succeeded.

During the siege Charles was taken ill at the house of Sir Hugh Patterson of Bannockburn and was overcome with fever. It was here that began the entanglement with Clementina Walkinshaw – she was a niece of his host, who nursed him in his illness – that was to go far in the completion of his ruin. It is probable that she was his mistress even in these early days and that he sought consolation for his bitter disappointments in her arms. It is certain that five or six year later she joined him in his exile, to his final undoing and her own.

While here too he was joined by the army from Perth and reinforced by four thousand men.

On 8 January the town of Stirling capitulated, although the castle successfully resisted all attempts at its capture. Disputes between the prince and Lord George Murray had by now become acute, Charles claiming sole control of the army and his lieutenant-general demanding that all orders should be given only after a council of war. Meanwhile an army of eight thousand English troops under General Hawley – an officer with an unenviable reputation for brutality to a beaten enemy – set out to the relief of Stirling and were met at Falkirk on 18 January. Once again England's best troops were routed by an impetuous army of Highlanders numerically smaller than their own.

The advantage thus gained, however, was immediately nullified by lack of generalship in pressing home the victory and by the inordinate love of plunder that prevented the undisciplined Highland army from consolidating its position and turning Hawley's defeat into a rout.

Lord George Murray's account of the action (recorded in Chambers's *Jacobite Memoirs of the Rebellion of 1745*) appears to lay the blame for this inability to press home his victory upon the prince for keeping the principal officers with him in the reserve and still more so for trusting O'Sullivan with the disposition of the troops. Murray states that he 'was never seen to do anything in the time of the action'.

The prince acted with his usual impetuous disregard of personal danger, and many accounts of the battle represent him as encouraging the men, but neither he nor Lord George Murray could restrain their inbred predilection for plundering their defeated enemies, and it is stated that out of an army five thousand strong the two together could scarce collect six hundred men for the pursuit.

The day after the battle a lamentable accident occurred that robbed the prince of many of his small force. Firing a shot in that spirit of recklessness and bravado that was common to many of the clansmen, one of the MacDonalds of Keppoch accidentally mortally wounded young Aeneas MacDonnell of Glen Garry, the second son of the chief of that clan. Prince Charles was frequently with the wounded lad and received his earnest prayer that his thoughtless slayer should be spared but was powerless to prevent the blood feud that arose, and the MacDonald was later executed for his careless act. Charles was heartbroken at the loss of his favourite 'Aide', and his grief at his death is recorded by several writers. The death-bed scene was graphically and romantically described in a *Scotland's Heir*, by Winifred Duke, where, however, the prince's character received less than justice at the author's hands.

At dawn on the following day young Glengarry's slayer paid the penalty for his carelessness, and shortly afterwards many of the MacDonalds deserted to their homes as a result. The attrition thus started spread to other clans. Lochgarry gives the total number of the MacDonalds at the Battle of Falkirk as two thousand one hundred and seventy-one, and other clans as two thousand four hundred and fifty, but in the account of his young kinsman's death, written to Glengarry, he states that 'there was a general desertion in the whole army' a few days later.

This went on for several days while the futile siege of Stirling Castle still continued, until, on 29 January, Lord George Murray sent the prince a letter signed by most of the Highland chiefs, including Lochiel, Keppoch, Clanranald, Lochgarry and the Master of Lovat, requesting His Royal Highness to retire to the Highlands on the grounds of the hourly desertions and suggesting a renewed campaign in the spring, asserting also that if the promised French help arrived meanwhile the Highlanders would immediately rise.

Poor, unhappy prince! He had no alternative but

to acquiesce. John Hay of Restalrig, who was the officer in attendance on the prince when the letter arrived early on the morning of 30 January, states in the appendix of John Home's[1] book, *History of the Rebellion in the Year 1745*, that when Charles received the letter he 'struck his head against the wall till he staggered, and exclaimed "Good God! that I have lived to see this day!"'

Hay is not always reliable, as, for instance, he states that no council was held at Derby whereas we have a direct account of such a council in Lochgarry's narrative, but in this case Hay's description of the scene is probably correct.

Charles appears to have replied immediately in perhaps the most poignant letter he ever penned, and if ever a document shows the heartbreak and despair to which a man can be reduced, it is that which is here reproduced as evidence that Charles Edward was as thorough in his argument as he was in his disregard of his personal comfort and danger throughout the whole campaign. Of necessity he bows to the decision conveyed in the letter, but in the penulti-

---

[1] John Home himself, as a lieutenant in a Glasgow regiment of volunteers took part in the Battle of Falkirk on the Hanoverian side. With some of his comrades he was taken prisoner and held at Doune Castle from which he organized a daring escape.

mate paragraph of his reply he voices his last despair-
ing hope that the matter may be reconsidered. His
letter runs as follows:

'BANNOCKBURN, *Jan. the 30th.*
'GENTLEMEN – I have received yrs. of last night and
am extremely surprised at the contents of it wch. I
little expected of you at this time.

'Is it possible that a victory and a defeat shoud pro-
duce the same effects and that the conquerors shoud
flie from an engagement whilst the conquered are
seeking it? Should we make the retreat you propose,
how much more will that raise the spirits of our
ennemys and sink those of our own people? Can we
imagine that where we go the ennemy will not follow and at last oblige us to a battel which we now
decline?

'Can we hope to defend ourselves at Perth, or keep
our men together there better than we do here? We
must therefore continue our flight to the mountains,
and soon find ourselves in a worse condition than we
were in at Glenfinnen. What opinions will the French
and Spaniards then have of us, or what encouragement will it be to the former to make the descent for
which we have been so long preparing, or the latter
to send us any more succours?

'I am persuaded that if the descent be not made before this piece of news reaches them, they will lay

aside all thoughts of it, cast all the blame upon us, and say it is vain to send succours to those who dare not stay to receive them. Will they send us any more artillery to be lost or naild up? But what will become of our Lowland friends? Shall we persuade them to retire with us to the mountains? Or shall we abandon them to the fury of our merciless ennemies?

'What an encouragement this will be to them or others to rise in our favour should we, as you seem to hope, ever think ourselves in a position to pay them a second visit? But besides what urges us to this precipitate resolution is, as I apprehend, the daily threats of the ennemy to come and attack us; and if they should do it within two or three days our retreat will become impracticable. For my own part I must say that it is with the greatest reluctance that I can bring myself to consent to such a step, but having told you my thoughts upon it, I am too sensible of what you have already ventured and done for me not to yield to yr. unanimous resolution if you persist in it.

'However I must insist on the conditions wch. Sr. Thomas Sheridan, the bearer of this, has my orders to propose to you. I desire you woud talk the matter over with him and give entire credit to what he shall say to you in my name. – Your assured friend.'

On receipt of this letter Sheridan returned with two of the principal chieftains, MacDonald of Keppoch and MacPherson of Cluny, to discuss the matter personally with the prince. Charles responded with an even stronger letter, reiterating his points and objections to a retreat, and through it his disappointment runs like a searing flame:

'I doubt not you have . . . heard great complaints of my despotick temper.

'I cant see nothing but ruin and destruction to us all. . . .

'Why shoud we be so much afraid now of an ennemy that we attacked and beat a fortnight ago when they were so much more numerous? . . .

'I know I have an army yt. I cannot command any further than the chief officers please. . . .

'If you are resolved upon it I must yield but I take God to witness that it is with the greatest reluctance, and that I wash my hands of the fatal consequences wch. I forsee but cannot help.'

In the light of these documents how anyone – and there have been many ready to do so – can charge Charles Edward with deserting his men after Culloden is incomprehensible. How truly indeed he foresaw the fatal consequences of which he washed his hands. Better, far better, for the chiefs and for the clans they led had they listened to his protests and met their fate south of the Forth as he wished. The result might possibly have been the same but at least they would have stood with a fresh and recently victorious army instead of with one worn out with privation, with ever-increasing desertions as the clans marched over the Highland roads – often deep in snow – that told them they were coming home and called to them with an insistence that many of them could not resist.

It was not to be. On 1 February the retreat began, and on the 2nd the council decided on their usual plan of dividing the army into two forces, the smaller, consisting of the Lowland regiments and the cavalry under Lord George Murray, taking the coast road through Montrose and Aberdeen, and the prince with the clans to take the formidable Highland road, both columns to make Inverness their final objective.

Once more the Fords of Frew witnessed the crossing of the Highland army – but how different in spirit from the crossing five months before.

On 2 and 3 February the prince was at Fairnton, the residence of Lord John Drummond, and from that house he dispatched Cluny Macpherson in advance to Badenoch with a commission to induce and compel recruits, with special powers of 'fire and sword' to all who might refuse. This commission still exists and, as is the case with all similar existing commissions, it is sealed with the royal arms of England and bears the usual preamble:

CHARLES PRINCE OF WALES &c. REGENT OF SCOTLAND ENGLAND FRANCE AND IRELAND AND THE DOMINIONS THEREUNTO BELONGING.

'To our trusty and well-beloved Evan McPherson of Cluny, Esq.

'These are empowering you to enlist in arms for our service all the men you possibly can whom you are to bring with all despatch to our army where we shall happen to be for the time, and they shall receive all manner of encouragement from us, but if any of the said persons shall refuse or delay to rise with you as aforesaid, we hereby authorize you to use all manner of military execution against their persons and effects, by burning their houses, destroying their cattle and further by these presents empower and require you to judge (or appoint a court martial for that purpose) all deserters from the regiment whom you are to punish by death or otherwise as to you or the said court martial shall appear just or reasonable, and lastly we hereby declare that these presents are without prejudice to an order issued by us at Carlisle the 19th November last namely that no Colonel of a regiment

91

receive or take any men from another corps which is again ratified and confirmed by us.

'Given at Fairntoun the 3rd day of February 1746.

CHARLES P. R.'

At Crieff the columns divided, Murray and his Lowlanders making for Perth and the coast, and the prince, as ever at the head of his clans, to the left through the romantic Sma' Glen by Amulree and Aberfeldy to Blair Atholl, where he slept in the castle four nights.

The Duke of Cumberland, who was now in command in Scotland and was gathering his forces for the pursuit, reached Perth on the same day that the prince arrived at Blair Atholl.

On 11 February Charles reached Dalwhinnie. By Glentruim he next arrived at the Spey. He spent the two following nights in Badenoch, and on 15 February was at Inverlaidnan, the house of Grant of Dalrachny. On 16 February he reached Moy Hall, where he was received by Lady MacIntosh, whose husband had joined the government. The same night Lord Loudoun sent a force of fifteen hundred men to surprise and capture the prince, but once again stratagem and cleverness succeeded, and Lady MacIntosh with a few retainers (the blacksmith of Moy, Fraser, and three or four men) defeated this comparatively large force at the 'Rout of Moy' and drove them back to Inverness. Even this was not disgrace enough for the gallant Lord Loudoun, and as the prince, having received reinforcements of a few hundred men, marched forward to Inverness, Loudoun hastily evacuated the town, leaving only a small garrison in the castle under Grant of Rothiemurchus, which was in as hopeless a position as the Jacobite garrison at Carlisle and surrendered on 20 February but met with much more humane treatment from their enemies.

Meanwhile Lord George Murray, leaving garrisons to keep open the roads to the coast, had joined Charles on 19 February at Culloden House, where many relics of the prince's visit remained for many years until they were finally dispersed by auction in the late nineteenth century.

Cumberland was now hot on Murray's trail. Aberdeen had been evacuated on 23 February after a few French troops had been landed and two days later had been occupied by the Duke of Cumberland's advance guard.

The prince visited the garrison at Elgin and appears to have been ill there for several days. His secretary, John Murray of Broughton, also became very ill there and left the prince's service for ever, to cover himself later with contempt for his betrayal of his master's secrets in order to save his own neck.

John Hay of Restalrig succeeded Murray as secretary to the prince, and although he seems to have been a loyal and devoted servant in that capacity, he earned the bitter censure of Lord George Murray as an utterly incompetent commissariat officer, a duty that also devolved upon him from his predecessor. The point need not be laboured, but he certainly seems to have left the entire army without food, even the officers receiving only a biscuit each on the night before the Battle of Culloden, while there was actually an abundance of provisions for a fortnight in the town of Inverness, only six or seven miles away.

The prince's chief officers achieved gallant and remarkable successes in many directions, but the very nature of these operations was fatal to the cause, for the little army was greatly weakened by the detailing of the troops necessary for the various projects.

It is evident that discussions between Charles and Lord George Murray took place in the interval between the latter's arrival at Culloden House on 19 February and the prince's departure on 3 March to Inverness, where he stayed in the house of the Dowager Lady MacIntosh, that were to have far-reaching and, in the end, disastrous consequences.

Dr Blaikie says that the prince had three things in view:

1 to reduce Fort Augustus and Fort William;
2 to disperse Lord Loudoun's army;
3 to keep possession of the road to Aberdeen as the only means of obtaining supplies.

The first project partially succeeded, and Fort Augustus surrendered on 5 March. Fort William held out and repulsed the attacking force with some loss, so that the troops rejoined the army at Inverness in good time to take part in the Battle of Culloden.

The dispersal of Lord Loudoun's army was a complete success, and the Duke of Perth's victorious troops were also released in time to participate in the final catastrophe, while Lord Loudoun fled to the Isle of Skye and took no part in the subsequent proceedings.

An interesting document showing the steps taken to secure the defeat of Lord Loudoun has been preserved:

'To Ewan McPherson Esqr of Cluny.
'SR, – Lady McIntosh desires you may raise all the McIntoshes men in Badenoch nothing but the hurry she was in hindered her from writing to you.

'His Royal Highness has just now received intelligence that Lord Loudoun march'd last night att twelve a clock the Fort Augustus road. Expresses were sent of to advertise Glengary and Cappoch [Keppoch] to intercept them but lest they should attempt Curryvareek [Corrieyairack Pass] His Highness desires you may immediately gett all your people together & give them a meeting on the hill. Don't neglect the moment you receive this to sent two three cleaver fellows to have certain intelligence of their motions. – I am, my dr sr,

JOHN MURRAY.'

The final project was apparently the most important and actually a disaster to the Jacobite prospects. The road to Aberdeen was already threatened by Cumberland's advancing army, but a large force under Lord John Drummond was dispatched to hold the line of the River Spey. Another force under Lord George Murray was detailed for the reduction of the English posts on the Highland road between Ruthven and Blair Castle. Cluny Macpherson was at Ruthven, holding the passes in Badenoch, and to him the prince dispatched a special courier with an important verbal message on 29 February. Doubtless his instructions were to work in cooperation with Lord George Murray, and the credentials of the messenger, entirely in the handwriting of the prince himself, on vellum, are preserved. They were evidently written in some haste and read as follows:

'The 29th Feby. 1746.
'I desire you will give entier credit to everything the bearer says to you from me. For Cluny Macpherson.
CHARLES P. R.'

Having evidently given the prince's messenger the 'entier credit' asked for by the prince, Cluny awaited some intimation from Lord George at his headquarters at Ruthven and on 11 March received the following letter:

'The Honble Collonell Macfearson of Clunie at or near Ruthven.
'SR, – I am now to acquaint you that I will be at Aviemore, or at a publick house at the Kirk of Alvie tomorow being Wednesday the 12th, by three a clock in the afternoon. The Atholl men are to come up the country by the way of Nairn & Cadle tomorow night so I wish you could fix upon a proper quartermaster. The pretence for our goeing up that country is to take a finall resolution with the Grants, & be at a point with them. I shall be very desirous to see you & Sheen tomorow at Aviemore, or near the Kirk of Alvie; at the same time I would wish my comming to

that country were as little known as could be, &
when known only as come to treat with the Grants. I
pray you have trusty men on all the passages towards
Atholl that none of the Grants or others may pass to
give intelegence. – I am dr. sr,

'Your most obedient humble servant

GEORGE MURRAY.'

The result was that Cluny and his MacPhersons
united forces with Lord George's Atholl men on 12
March, and on the 17th the two commanders surprised and captured no fewer than thirty of the government's posts without loss and proceeded to be-
siege Blair Atholl Castle, where much valuable time
was lost, the siege being abandoned on 2 April. Lord
George was able to make a hurried journey to Inverness in time to participate at Culloden on the 16th,
but some of the Atholl men got no farther than the
Grant country on the Spey, while Cluny returned to
Badenoch for further orders and the MacPhersons
had the mortification of arriving in haste within six
miles of the battlefield on the fatal 16 April, only to
hear that all was lost.

The posts captured by Cluny and Lord George included Blairfetty, Kenichan, Glendulichan and
Cochivile in Rannoch, which were under the command of Captain Campbell of Knockbowie with

two hundred and twenty men of the Argyllshire militia, and amongst the baggage and effects that were captured by Cluny Macpherson was a direct order dated from Nairn House on 20 February 1746, which disposes of the suggestion that the cruelties and slaughters after Culloden were only in retaliation for similar orders given by the prince to his troops before the same battle. Captain Campbell's written orders were as follows:

'*Orders for Captain Campbell of Knockbowie.*
'You are to march directly hence with your own Company, Carsaig's, Raschellys, and Ardmenish's to the following parts where you are to dispose of them as follows:
'At Blairfetty .... 60 men
'At Kenichan .... 100 men
'(Where you are to be yourself).
'At Glendulichan and Cochiville .... 60 men
   'It is the Duke of Cumberland's orders that you take post according to the above list.
   'You are to command the several companies above mentioned.
   'Such of the rebels as may be found in arms you are to take prisoners, and if any of them make resistance, you are to attack them, provided their numbers do not exceed yours. And it is his royal highness's orders that you give them no quarters.

'You are to seize upon all kind of provisions that belongs to the rebels or may be designed for their use.

'You are to make your report three times a week to the Commanding Officer at Castle Menzies or Blair of Atholl.

(Signed) JOHN CAMPBELL.'

On 25 March the army suffered a serious loss in the recapture by the English of the *Hazard* sloop in the Pentland Firth, with one hundred and forty-six men and twelve thousand pounds in money which she had brought from France. Fifteen hundred men under Lord Cromarty were detailed to attempt to recover the gold but were surprised and defeated by a Hanoverian clan (the MacKays). Cromarty was captured and the rest of the force returned too late to take part in the final battle.

On 8 April, his preparations complete, Cumberland began his march, crossed the Spey on the 13th, the Atholl men retreating before him, and marched into Nairn as the Duke of Perth marched out. The latter joined Prince Charles and his attenuated army at Culloden House, which was now his headquarters.

In the interim Charles had done everything possible to keep up the spirits of his men and his supporters in Inverness. He shook off his depression, and Maxwell of Kirkconnell says that 'he appeared gayer even than usual, gave frequent balls to the ladies of Inverness, and danced himself, which he had declined doing at Edinburgh in the midst of his grandeur and gaiety.'

This is eloquent tribute to the gallant spirit of the man who two months before had 'washed his hands of the fatal consequences which he foresaw, but could not help'. But he knew that the hour of his fate was approaching. His army was reduced to fewer than five thousand men owing to the other expeditions already referred to, so that although he was hourly expecting the return of Cromarty's force of fifteen hundred and had summoned Cluny MacPherson and his clan from Badenoch, he was well aware that an attack by a fresh and trained army of nearly ten thousand men might be expected at any moment.

On 15 April a night attack upon the Duke of Cumberland's resting army was planned, which, with one more hour of darkness, might have turned the whole fortunes of the cause and, indeed, of the kingdom. It was Cumberland's birthday, and it was almost certain that the occasion would be considered one for convivial celebration.

The council met. An immediate forced march and attack were proposed by the prince himself, and – for once almost unanimously – he was supported by Lord George Murray and his chief officers.

The objective was some twelve miles as the crow flies, but the attacking force had to march by night across difficult country and delays were inevitable. At about four o'clock in the morning they were still three miles from the duke's camp, when, for some inexplicable reason, Lord George decided that the attack could not be delivered with any hope of success and ordered a retirement. Lord George himself seems to have thought that daylight would make defeat certain.

Charles, many years afterwards, informed John Home, the historian, that he rode up to Lord George to inquire the reason for the halt and was convinced of the necessity for retreating. Hay of Restalrig states that when first he heard that a retreat had been ordered, Charles exclaimed that he had been betrayed by Lord George, which, with his constant doubts and suspicions of his principal general, may well have been his opinion.

Whatever the facts, at six o'clock in the morning Charles was back at Culloden House, and the army, utterly worn out with a night march of over twenty miles, faint with hunger and fatigue, threw themselves on the sodden heather of Drumossie Moor and slept – many of them their last sleep in life. Some, indeed, never awakened until the battle was over, and Sir Robert Strange says, 'Over a thousand were asleep in Culloden parks during the action.'

CHAPTER IV

*T*HE BATTLE OF
CULLODEN

In his *Itinerary*, Dr Blaikie rightly states that the most graphic account of the night march to Nairn and the Battle of Culloden is given by the artist and engraver Sir Robert Strange, and as his personal narrative also contains the sole account of the engraving of a special plate for notes with which to pay the troops, which was completed two days before the battle, it is possible to rely upon his account for the description of the final extinction of the Jacobite cause at the Battle of Culloden Moor.

The plate for the notes that Strange engraved was evidently hastily buried by the flying 'treasurer' immediately after the battle. It bears an inscription that it was 'found buried in the ground near Loch Laggan about the year 1860'.

The *Memoirs of Sir Robert Strange* has the following narrative:

'During this period that the army were stationed in and about Inverness, the first battalion of the Life Guards, commanded by Lord Elcho, were billeted upon Culloden House. One evening, after I had retired to rest, an express arrived from Inverness between eleven and twelve, acquainting me that the Prince was desirous of seeing me as soon as possible. I that instant got up, and my horse being saddled, I made the best of my way to town. Upon my being announced at the headquarters, I was desired to be shown into the Prince's bedchamber. There was this evening a ball. After having waited but a short time, the Prince, accompanied by Sir Thomas Sheridan, and Mr Murray, the secretary, came into the room. Sir Thomas Sheridan took the lead, and addressing himself to me more particularly, told me that His Royal Highness was desirable of taking my opinion, relating to a circulation of one species of money or another, which it had been thought expedient to issue for the service of the army in general, but more particularly amongst the soldiery, and that they were desirous of knowing what plan I could recommend as the most eligible. I answered Sir Thomas that the subject was new to me; that, so far as regarded my own profession, I thought everything of the kind exceedingly practicable; but that it was a question with me whether or not the town of Inverness could afford me what assistance would be necessary in executing a work of this kind, particularly a rolling press, which would be indispensable on the occasion; but, if they would indulge me with a few hours the next day, I should then have put my thoughts together upon the subject, have considered it in every point of view, and give my opinion of course. It was agreed upon that I should return the next evening between eight and nine.

'I attended soon after eight, and was again shown into the same apartment as I had been the night before. Soon after the Prince appeared, accompanied as the preceding evening, with the addition of a third gentleman. Sir Thomas Sheridan again accosted me, and asked me what I had done. I answered, that it was just as I had apprehended, for that there was no such thing in the town of Inverness as a rolling press; but, that I had had recommended me a very intelligent man of a carpenter, and an excellent mechanic, who had entered into my ideas, and perfectly comprehended the construction of what was required, and was even ready to begin such, were it necessary. I then proceeded towards explaining what I had in view, and with that intention pulled out of my pocket a small device which I had put together, the better to communicate my ideas. It consisted, I said, of nothing but the slightest compartment, from behind which a rose issued on one side, and a thistle on the other, as merely ornamental; the interior part I meant should be filled up by clerks, with the specific sums which were intended, etc.; and I proposed etching or engraving, in the slightest manner for expedition, a considerable repetition of this ornament on two plates, for the facility of printing; that such should be done on the strongest paper (so) that, when cut separate, they should resist, in some measure, the wear they must sustain in the common use of circulation. The Prince had at this time taken the compartment out of my hand, and was showing (it) to Mr Murray, and seemed much pleased with the idea of the rose and the thistle. In short, everything was approved of, and the utmost expedition recommended me.

'We now talked of a circulation of larger sums, which would likewise be required. I gave it as my opinion, that I thought they could not do better than issue notes in imitation of the Bank of England, or the Royal Bank of Scotland, in the execution of which there was very little labour; that it would be necessary, if possible, to see such notes, in order to concert a form how they were to be drawn up, by whom paid, or at what period; if at a given time, that of the Restoration I imagined would be the properest. This produced a general smile. Mr Murray at this instant left the room, and, soon after returning on his steps, brought with him two notes of the Bank of England, one for one hundred pounds, and the other for two, and which, though different in appearance, yet both were payable on demand. On examining those notes I observed the impossibility of having a proper paper made for the occasion, but that I did imagine the finest post paper would be sufficiently adequate for the purpose; that it had strength enough, as the notes would be less subject to friction in the wear than the smaller paper, which would be in circulation amongst the soldiery. All this was agreed upon, and Mr Murray said, as I would have occasion for the notes to regulate me in the engraving, I might then put them in my pocket, and that in the course of a few days I should hear from them, when they had considered of a proper form for drawing up what was intended. The Prince, on my leaving the room, recommended me all diligence.

'Next day, being Sunday, my carpenter was early employed in cutting out his wood, in order to begin on Monday. It was not so with a coppersmith, whose assistance I more immediately required. He was a good Presbyterian, and thought he would be breaking the Lord's Day. But necessity has no law; he turned out even better than his promise, overcame his prejudice, went to work, and furnished me with a copper plate on Monday about noon. I had passed that morning in making a composition of etching varnish, but had not perfectly proportioned the materials, for I well recollect the aqua-fortis playing the devil with it, but which was repaired with some little trouble. In short, it mattered not much, provided the purpose was answered; and, indifferent as things might be, I would at this moment purchase a series of them even at a considerable expense, to decorate as it were this volume with the more juvenal works of its author. Such would be a curiosity of the kind. The reader may naturally conclude that, on this occasion, I lost not a single hour. Solicitous in the service in which I was employed, my activity was, of course, redoubled; I laboured till late at night, and waited the approach of day with impatience. Not a fortnight had elapsed when I was ready to begin printing, and had even forwarded the notes for a larger circulation.

'Such was the position of my undertaking when, all of a sudden, news was brought to Inverness that the Duke of Cumberland, with his army, had passed the Spey on the 13th of April. The town was in a general alarm, and even in confusion. Nothing was heard but the noise of bagpipes, the beating of drums, and the clash of arms. The field of Culloden was the following day to be the general rendezvous, and every individual betook himself to his corps.

'The next morning I went betimes to the Secretary's office, and delivered over the whole of my charge, together with the notes I had been entrusted with. I told the treasurer that an account would be presented by a carpenter who had been very active in serving me; that there would be added to it a few articles he had disbursed, and requested the whole might be paid; which was accordingly done. I now returned to Culloden House. My companions were, in general, glad to see me, and, joking, asked me when they were to have any of my money. I replied that, if they gave a good account of the Duke, I hoped his treasury chest would supply us.

'The army was now mustering upon the field, it being the 14th; but unfortunately we had not been joined by a considerable number of our men, who were actually upon their march from different parts of the country, and would have been up in the course of a few days. The whole of the MacPhersons, a considerable body of the Frasers, some few of the Macintoshes, in general all the MacKenzies, and several other bodies of men who had been raised in the more northern counties, had all received repeated expresses, and were hastening to join the army. In this situation, divested as it were of part of our numbers, we hourly expected the Duke. He had come on to Nairn on the 14th, and was there halting. There was even no appearance of his moving, the 15th being his birthday. In the afternoon of that day, the Prince had summoned a council of war to be held upon the field, and had proposed a plan of a march under cloud of night, to attack the Duke's army by surprise, and to force his camp. This plan was worthy even of any of the greatest heroes of antiquity, and met with general approbation, particularly amongst the clans. The council remained long in deliberating in what manner it was to be conducted. Two essential things, secrecy and expedition, were the great objects to be observed. There was only one road to Nairn, which was the high road; and this being covered in many places with villages, it was essential to avoid it, to prevent any information being carried to the Duke's army. The next alternative, and indeed the only one, was to attempt a way along the foot of a ridge of mountains which fronted the sea, but had scarcely been ever trode by human foot, and was known by the name of the Moor-road. It would have brought us in upon that part of the enemy's camp from which they could apprehend no danger. It lengthened indeed the road, which, in sequel, and from the shortness of the night, proved our misfortune.

'Before the council broke up, every regiment as it were had his place assigned him in the order of the march. The van was commanded by Lord George Murray, who, with about one-third of the army, was to have passed the water of Nairn about two miles distant from the town, and who, unexpected by the enemy, was to have invested the Duke's forces, and to have made him prisoner. The remaining two-thirds, commanded by the Duke of Perth and Lord John Drummond, were to have attacked them from the plain, which, in all probability, would have been carried sword in hand. It is to be remarked that the same army had been already surprised at Falkirk.

'Night coming on – and not sooner could the army begin its march, to prevent the country people from being alarmed, or any intelligence being carried to the enemy – part of our numbers, weak as we were, was under a necessity of being left on the field, in order to save appearances, and light up fires, as had been done the preceding evening, and to prevent stragglers, if any there were, forming unnecessary conjectures. The night was favourable to our wishes, but, alas! such a road was never travelled; the men in general were frequently up to the ankles, and the horses in many places extricated themselves with difficulty. In this manner were we retarded almost the whole of the night; notwithstanding of which, an uncommon spirit supported itself throughout the army.

'It was now the 16th of April, when day began to break about four in the morning. It was indeed a dreadful knell to us, being as yet above four long miles from Nairn; nor did we know what sort of road we had yet to encounter. Appearances became serious, each was whispering to his neighbour, and so far as countenances could be described, disappointment was evidently marked. During this critical moment of suspense, what was to be done? A halt took place. A council was called as soon as the general officers could be got together. The morning was fine and the day was ushering in apace; it required but little time to deliberate, and finding it impossible to attack the Duke by surprise, it was judged expedient for the safety of the army to give up the enterprise and return to the field of Culloden. Thus were our hopes disappointed. We saw, as it were before us, the glorious prize; but we durst not encounter it, for there is almost a moral certainty that we should have been cut off to a man. The enemy was early in motion, must have seen us at a considerable distance, and received us upon the points of their bayonets.

'We now turned about to the left, and as soon as we conveniently could, got into the high road. The Prince, attended by followers and a few of his body-guards, went on towards Culloden. Thus did the shortness of the night, attended with a most harassing march, prevent a plan from being carried into execution which was as morally certain of success as it would have been glorious to the youth who projected it. For it is a known truth that the enemy had no idea of the intended attack, and that the first information they received was after their army had begun to move; and it was even communicated to them from their own vanguard, who had learnt it upon their march. We had got but a few miles upon the road, when a number of the guards, finding themselves overpowered with fatigue, and ready every instant to drop from our saddles, came to a resolution of stopping: we were shown into an open barn, where we threw ourselves down upon some straw, tying our horses to our ankles, and the people assuring us that, in case of any danger, they should awake us. They were indeed as good as their promise, for we had slumbered here but a short time before a woman gave us the alarm that the Duke's horse were in sight. We that instant mounted; and as soon as we got upon the high road, the vanguard, as yet at some distance, were approaching. We now made the best of our way; but, before ascending to the field, we found the Prince had been there some time, and was actually at that moment engaged in holding a council of war, deliberating whether we should give battle to the Duke, or, circumstanced as the army was, retire and wait the arrival of our reinforcements. The former was determined on.

'Let us for an instant view the situation of this army. They had, for many weeks before the battle, been reduced to a short allowance of bread; when I say bread, I mean oatmeal, for they had no other. Must not this have enfeebled their bodies? Their treasury chest had been nearly exhausted: they had received but little money: of course considerable arrears were owing them. They had passed the 14th and following night under arms upon the field of battle, every instant expecting the Duke. Upon the night of the 15th, which was the eve of the battle, they had performed the march I have described. Judge then, what was to be expected of such an army, worn out with fatigue, and at this moment short of the common necessaries of life, and outnumbered upwards of two to one by their enemies; for the Duke's army consisted of at least eleven thousand men; that of the Prince did not exceed six, of which we shall find at least a thousand during the action were asleep in Culloden parks. What, then, can justify the deliberate folly and madness of fighting under such circumstances? But our time was come. We were at variance within ourselves: Irish intriguers and French politics were too predominant in our councils. These gentlemen, forsooth, considered themselves as to be but prisoners of war, whilst every other individual were fighting with halters round their necks. General appearances upon the field of battle were much against us. No line was as yet formed, the men were standing in clusters; and stragglers in small numbers were coming up from all quarters. Overpowered with fatigue, they had stopped everywhere on the road, and were now joining the army.

'It being determined to give battle to the Duke, no time was now lost in forming the lines, and in making every proper disposition. The right of the army, commanded by Lord George Murray, was composed of his own regiment of Atholl, the Camerons, Stewarts of Appin, one battalion of the Frasers, and the Macin-

115

toshes. The left wing, commanded by the Duke of Perth, consisted of the MacDonalds of Glen Garry, Keppoch, and Clanranald, two companies of Mac-Leans, two of MacLeods, and the Farquharsons. The second line, commanded by Lord John Drummond and Major-General Stapleton, consisted of the Irish pickets, the regiments of Lord Ogilvy, Lord Lewis Gordon, Duke of Perth, and Lord John Drummond. On the right wing, behind the second line, was a troop of Fitz-James' horse, and on the left part of the horse-guards, Perthshire squadron, and hussars. The regiment of Kilmarnock's foot-guards, and Colonel John Roy Stewart, with such of the men as had no guns, formed a sort of reserve. The Prince, attended by his aides-de-camp, and Lord Elcho's guards, placed himself towards the centre; behind the first line. We had six pieces of cannon; two placed on the right, two on the left, and two in the centre of the front line.

'The Duke of Cumberland drew up his army in three lines. The first, commanded by Lieutenant-General the Earl of Albemarle, consisted of the regiments of Burrel, Monro, Scot's Fusiliers, Price, Cholmondley, and St Clair. The second, commanded by Major-General Huske, consisted of the regiments of Wolfe, Ligonier, Sempill, Bligh, and Fleming. The third line, commanded by Brigadier Mordaunt, consisted of the regiments of Blanckney, Battereau, Pultney, and Howard. On the right wing were placed Cobham's dragoons, and the other half of Kingston's horse, with the Campbells of Argyll. Ten pieces of cannon were placed in the first, line, two between each regiment, and six pieces in the second line.

'The enemy formed at a considerable distance, and marched on in order of battle, outlining us both on the right and on the left. About one o'clock the cannonading began; and the Duke's artillery being well served, could not fail of doing execution. One of the Prince's grooms, who led a sumpter horse, was killed upon the spot; some of the guards were wounded, as were several of the horse. One Austin, a very worthy, pleasant fellow, stood on my left; he rode a fine mare, which he was accustomed to call his lady. He perceived her give a sudden shrink, and, on looking around him, called out, 'Alas! I have lost my lady!' One of her hind legs was shot, and hanging by the skin. He that instant dismounted, and, endeavouring to push her out of the ranks, she came to the ground. He took his gun and pistols out of the holsters, stepped forward, joined the foot, but was never more heard of. The Prince, observing this disagreeable position, and without answering any end whatever, ordered us down to a covered way, which was a little towards our right, and where we were less annoyed with the Duke's cannon: he himself, with his aides-de-camps, rode along the line towards the right, animating the soldiers. The guards had scarce been a minute or two in this position, when the small arms began from the Duke's army, and kept up a constant fire; that instant, as it were, one of the aides-de-camp returned, and desired us to join the Prince. We met him in endeavouring to rally the soldiers, who, annoyed with the enemy's fire, were beginning to quit the field. The right of our army, commanded by Lord George Murray, had made a furious attack, cut their way through Burrel's and Monro's regiments, and had taken possession of two pieces of cannon; but a reinforcement of Wolfe's regiment, &c., coming up from the Duke's second line, our right wing was obliged to give way, being at the same time flanked with some pieces of artillery, which did great execution. Towards the left the attack had been less vigorous than on the right, and of course had made but little impression on the Duke's army. Nor was it indeed general, for the centre, which had been much galled by the enemy's artillery, almost instantly quitted the field.

'The scene of confusion was now great; nor can the imagination figure it. The men in general were betaking themselves precipitately to flight; nor were there any possibility of their being rallied. Horror and dismay were painted in every countenance. It now became time to provide for the Prince's safety: his person had been abundantly exposed. He was got off the field, and very narrowly escaped falling in with a body of horse, which had been detached from the Duke's left, were advancing with an incredible rapidity, picking up the stragglers, and, as they gave no quarter, were levelling them with the ground. The great numbers of the army were already out of danger, the flight having been so precipitate. We got upon a rising ground, where we turned round and made a general halt. The scene was, indeed, tremendous. Never was so total a rout – a more thorough discomfiture of an army. The adjacent country was in a manner covered with its ruins. The whole was over in about twenty-five minutes. The Duke's artillery kept still playing, though not a soul upon the field. His army was kept together, all but the horse. The great pursuit was upon the road towards Inverness. Of towards six thousand men, which the Prince's army at this period consisted of, about one thousand were asleep in Culloden parks, who knew nothing of the action till awaked by the noise of the cannon. These in general endeavoured to save themselves by taking the road towards Inverness; and most of them fell a sacrifice to the victors, for this road was in general strewed with dead bodies. The Prince at this moment had his cheeks bedewed with tears; what must not his feeling heart have suffered!'

The value of this clear narrative by an important eye-witness of the battle cannot be overestimated, and one may well rely upon it for a general description of the action itself. Many more elaborate accounts still, of course, exist, and some details have perhaps been given more than their due proportion by later writers.

One such was the relative positions of the 'Atholl men' under Lord George Murray and the Mac-Donalds under Lochgarry, Keppoch and Clanranald. It is certain that there was a dispute as to the hereditary right claimed by the MacDonalds to fight on the right wing, which they had worthily held during most, if not indeed all, of the previous engagements of the campaign. At Culloden Lord George Murray had claimed the position for his Atholl troops on the ground that they had occupied that position under the Duke of Montrose. This much is clear, for Lochgarry in his report to his chieftain, Glengarry, who was then a prisoner, writes:

'The MacDonnells had the left that day, the prince having agreed to give the right to Lord George and his Atholmen. Upon which Keppoch, Clanranald and I spoke to his R.Hs. upon the subject, and begged he woud allow us our former right, but he intreated us for his sake we woud not dispute it, as he had already agreed to give it to Ld. George and his Atholmen; and I heard H.R.Hs. say he ressented it very much, and should never doe the like if he had occasion for it.'

It is clear, therefore, that there was considerable feeling in the ranks of the MacDonalds at their removal from the right to the left flank, but there is hardly sufficient evidence to warrant the suggestion that has been made by many writers that the MacDonald clan actually refused to fight as a result.

Even so generally fair an historian as Andrew Lang appears to attach too much importance to a very unfortunate incident when he says that Lord George's advice 'made the injured MacDonalds no longer a force in being', and again later, in speaking of the delay in the attack by the left wing, 'how far their irresolution meant a military strike out of wrath at being placed on the left can never be certainly decided', but when he goes on to suggest that Clanranald's MacDonalds sullenly 'beheld the gallant but fatal attempt of the Camerons, Stewarts, Clans Chattan, MacLeans, and their own folk under Keppoch and Scothouse', he surely goes too far. Lochgarry's is a detailed and clear report, and it will be seen from the following extract that the MacLeans were immediately on the right of Lochgarry's regiment and lost one hundred and fifty out of two hundred men:

'Att this unlucky battle we were all on the left, and near to us on the right the brave McLeans who woud have been about 200 as well looked men as ever I saw, commanded by McLean of Drumnine, one of the prince's gentlemen of that clan; he and his son were both killd on the spot, and I believe 50 of that number did not come of the field. H.R.Hs. being close to our line in time of the action, and seeing at last such a totall deroute of his army, was obliged to retire. The horse he himself rode was shot under him, and one of his servants killed by his side with a cannon ball; he happend to have none of the leading people then by him, or anyone who knew the country well.'

From this it is not unreasonable to suppose:

1 that the MacDonalds under Clanranald were to be held in reserve;
2 that they were acting as some sort of bodyguard to the prince. It is surely contrary to all Highland tradition and experience to imagine that they would see 'their own folk under Keppoch and Scothouse' slaughtered, as Lang suggests.

Be this as it may, MacLean and MacDonald of Keppoch fell wounded and were slain where they fell. In twenty-five minutes all was over, and the remnant of the clans were in full flight, some on the road to Inverness, others across the Nairn Water towards the mountains.

Lochgarry says that the prince had ordered no rendezvous, but it is doubtful whether this is correct, as Captain O'Neil in his account says distinctly otherwise, and there is no question that Maxwell of Kirkconnel and Andrew Lang are correct in saying that when all was lost he sent a nephew of Sir Thomas Sheridan to lead some of the fugitives towards Ruthven and that Sheridan led them to suppose that he was conducting them to a place of re-assembly for the army in Badenoch. In any case, whatever orders were given seem to have been very confused and confusing, as was not unnatural in the difficult circumstances.

The pitiable scene after the battle beggars description. Cumberland had given orders that no quarter was to be given to the rebels, and they were murdered in hundreds, the wounded where they fell and such of the flying clansmen as were overtaken either on the road to Inverness or in the swamps and mosses of the Nairn by the pursuing English troops.

Lord George Murray fled to Ruthven to join Cluny, and from there wrote a bitter, upbraiding, sarcastic letter to Charles, blaming him for the entire rebellion from first to last and for landing at all without the aid of French troops, entirely overlooking his own acquiescence in all the decisions of the council in pressing the retreat from Falkirk to the Highlands, in originating the night march to Nairn, which was so important a factor in the loss of the battle the following day, and finally in insisting that the Atholl men should displace the MacDonalds on the right wing.

Lord George Murray was undoubtedly the ablest officer in the prince's service, but there can be no question that his dictatorial disposition and hectoring conduct to his prince and the Highland chieftains went far to cause the dissensions and disputes that so frequently occurred amongst the proud Highlanders, and the antipathy that Charles afterwards displayed towards his erstwhile major-general is indeed not to be wondered at. Having resigned before Carlisle in November 1745, he repeated his resignation in the letter from Ruthven on 17 April in terms that admit no excuse, although it is doubtful whether the letter ever reached the prince's hands.

Is it to be wondered at that, as Neil McEachain says, 'The prince claimed always Lord George as being the only instrument in losing the battle,' and that two years afterwards he wrote from Paris to his father, the Chevalier, on hearing that Lord George Murray was going to Rome, that 'it would be of the most dangerous consequences iff such a divill was not secured immediately in sum castle, where he might be at his ease, but without being able to escape.'

We can turn our attention at this point to examine the subsequent life of Prince Charles, and we can leave Lord George Murray and the controversy as to whether he or the prince was right or wrong to the historian and student of the events and possibilities of the attempt, and return to the scene of the slaughter at Culloden Moor.

Greatly as it has changed since the fatal day when the last of the Stuart princes made his final throw for the throne of his ancestors and lost – for the acceptance of his cardinal's hat by Henry, Duke of York, was a renunciation by that prince of any claim he might otherwise have had to the English crown – Culloden must always remain a place of intense interest to the visitor, whether of Highland or of English blood, and in the former case give rise to emotion and feelings that cannot be adequately described.

Let us try to reconstruct the scene on the afternoon of that fatal 16 April from its modern surroundings.

A rough cart track led up from the town of Inverness to the upper gates of Culloden parks over marshy and boggy ground. Dark, lowering clouds drifted across a leaden sky before a northwesterly wind that brought flurries of sleet and snow across the sodden ground at frequent intervals. On the left of the ascent lay the Moray Firth, with white-capped rollers running out to sea before the wind. Below was the moorland road and, between it and the sea, the fertile strath, with Culloden House, the headquarters of the Highland army the night before, seen between the sparse spruce, larch and fir trees of the park.

As the imaginary eyewitness climbs the winding road he passes on the left the barns in which the worn-out Life Guards stabled their horses and threw themselves down in utter exhaustion after the futile march to Nairn on the night before the battle and where more than one poor wounded and unarmed soul dragged himself to shelter after the defeat when iron-shod hoofs or a pistol bullet through the back had struck him down in the merciless pursuit of the English cavalry – lucky for those who were killed outright as they fled down the rough road. For him who lived and suffered, all that was left of life was beaten out by clubbed musket butts or slashed from the suffering body by a dozen bayonets when he was dragged, begging for his life, from his hiding place.

Upward still, the scene grows more horrible where the boggy moor opens out from the road. Scarcely a yard is free from the aftermath of the brutal and most pitiable 'victory' that ever stained British arms or from the shameful slaughter that will forever stain the memory of the royal 'Butcher'. Gleaming white in the fading light of the April afternoon, the mangled bodies of the slain suffered the last indignity of the ghouls who followed in the wake of the slaughtering cavalry and tore the last poor rags of a six months' campaign from the dead in their lust for plunder.

On the field itself now stands a huge cairn of stones not far from the spot where Prince Charles took his stand, near to the left-centre of the line, and where his horse was supposed to have been shot from under him. From this spot onwards to the east busy bands of soldiers were digging the long trenches that were to contain the bodies of the clansmen lying in swathes where they fell under fire. Over the field roamed the 'executioners', and a sharp report or a dull thud told where bullet or musket butt had scattered the brains of some poor unfortunate in whose body a little spark of life still survived. But even this act of mercy was withheld on the following morning when the searchers and slaughterers tired of their sport – why trouble or waste powder? The order was 'No quarter to the wounded' – what matter if some poor conscious wretch is bundled into the open trenches with his dead brothers? A few mouthfuls of his native peat served his turn just as well as knocking out his brains, so the few still living joined the happier dead in their last sleep upon Drummossie Moor.

A bubbling stream, dyed red in Highland blood and choked with Highland bodies, saved others trouble, and more yet were piled on them to sink into the ooze that is now the so well-named 'well of the dead'.

An eyewitness to these horrors was Ranald Mac-Donald of Belfinlay, who is stated by Bishop Forbes in his book *Lyon in Mourning* to have been:

'a Captain in the Highland Army, and had the misfortune to be shott through the two leggs in the action, which rendered him incapable to make his escape. He lay in a field after he received his wounds, and was betwixt the fire of the English Army and that of the few French troops that made some resistance after the Highlanders were routed, where showers of balls passed by him. He remained likewise in the field all that night after he was stript of all his cloaths, his very shirt and breeches being taken from him. But as he was young and of a robust constitution he lived till next morning, when he saw that cruell command coming to execute their bloody orders, and saw many of his unhappy companions putt to death in cold blood. They were just presenting their firelocks to his own breast when he was saved through the clemency of Lieutenant Hamilton, who, if he remembers, belonged to Cholmondley's regiment, and who took him to a neighbouring country house.'

Bishop Forbes had this account in his collection in Ranald MacDonald's own handwriting.

Close by, too, stands another record: 'Here Mac-Gillivray fell', well on towards the English lines and the fatal park wall from where Highlanders of the Campbell Clan poured a withering fire into their kilted brothers of Clans Chattan and MacDonald. Here the noble Keppoch had fallen, mortally wounded, trying still to struggle on, and was slaughtered where he fell.

Captain Donald Roy MacDonald has given a moving account of Keppoch's death:

'At the battle of Culloden in the retreat Captain Roy MacDonald saw Keppoch fall twice to the ground, and knows no more about him but that, upon the second fall, looking at Donald Roy MacDonald he

129

spoke these words: "O God have mercy upon me. Donald, do the best for yourself, for I am gone.'"

Still farther on stood the enclosing park wall with the great gaps from where the Campbells had pulled aside the stones to let out the English cavalry on their errand of murder once the flight had begun.

The trenches in which the bodies of the clansmen were buried on the night of and the day after the battle have since been marked by granite stones on which are carved the names of the occupants. The grave nearest Inverness was used for the Campbells killed in the battle on the government side, and the succeeding trenches are marked with the following clan names:

MacIntoshes	Stewarts of Appin
Frasers	MacLeans
MacGillivray	MacLachlans
Mixed Clans	Atholl Highlanders

A verse from a later rhyme is descriptive of the scene as it is today:

'MacGillivray true
The MacIntosh too,
Brave Stuart of Appin beneath a stone lies.
The Grant and the Fraser

130

Are under the heather,
And the hawk and the owl o'er their
  resting place flies.'

So perished all the high hopes, so ended the splendours of Edinburgh and the endurance and courage of the long march into England and of the great attempt against always increasing odds. In the peaty ooze of a Highland moor the Stuart cause lies buried forever, with the bodies of the clansmen dead for that cause and for a prince who was to survive, it is true, but who was to endure yet more suffering and hardship with the indomitable spirit, with the patient endurance and with the laughing recklessness that characterized him from first to last in the country of his ancestors before the bitterness of defeat and blighted hopes in an alien land turned his sunny disposition into despair and into the querulous misery of a debauched and unreasonable old man.

CHAPTER V

*E*SCAPE TO THE
HEBRIDES

Andrew Lang describes Charles in his wanderings as brave, enduring and contented, and says of him that 'it may even be held that he was happier when a proscribed wanderer than at any other time of his life.' His history, at least all that matters of it, draws towards its close. Dr Blaikie sets out a full account of his romantic journeyings in his *Itinerary*, but we can outline his general movements and his later years in so far as they reveal his character.

With 'his cheeks bedewed with tears', as Sir Robert Strange has narrated, Charles crossed the water of Nairn at the Ford of Failie but followed the right bank of the river to Aberarder and so by Loch Faroline to Gortleg, where the 'old fox', Lord Lovat, was awaiting events. From this stronghold he sent his message to Cluny MacPherson, and there is a conflict of opinion as to whether or not he expected the remnants of his army to meet him at Fort Augustus, which was still in his hands. However, he reached the fort on the night of the battle, a distance of over thirty miles of trackless moor, covered after two o'clock in the afternoon of an April day – a feat that indicates a very hurried flight.

Captain O'Neil in both copies of his *Journal* definitely states that 'previous to the battle the prince ordered the chieftains in case of a defeat, as the Highlanders could not retreat as regular troops, to assemble their men near Fort Augustus,' and as O'Neil was directly attached to the prince throughout the early days of his flight and accompanied him in his wanderings in the Western Islands, his narrative seems to be generally dependable, although in some details it is obviously inaccurate.

No troops arrived at Fort Augustus, and O'Neil was left there for two days to direct any who might arrive to follow His Royal Highness, but as he pathetically remarks, 'to no effect, everyone taking his own road'.

The deserted and now ruined Invergarry Castle was reached during the night, and, according to Bishop Forbes in *Lyon in Mourning,* the little party, rested until the following afternoon 'without meat,

133

drink, fire or candle, except some firr sticks and a salmon and gridiron bannocks', before following the northern shore of Loch Arkaig to Glen Pean. Utterly wearied, they passed the night in the heather-thatched home of Donald Cameron, from where they crossed the hills of Glen Morar and sheltered in a shieling near the River Meoble. Between there and Borradale the prince met Donald MacLeod, the pilot of the 'eight oarded boat', who proved such a loyal and trustworthy friend to his prince. Throughout Donald MacLeod's whole narrative to Bishop Forbes he insisted on using the titles 'His Majesty' or 'His Excellency' in his references to Prince Charles and showed a respect and an affection for his prince that was another remarkable testimony to the charm that could provoke such chivalrous devotion in a rough island fisherman who had no other knowledge of him or his family claims until he met him as a proscribed and hunted fugitive with a price on his head. Donald offered to guide him to the Hebrides in the hope of a vessel to France and told the prince he would do anything in the world for him.

The prince remained in hiding until a boat was procured on 26 April, when the little party sailed at night from Loch nan Uamh for the Outer Hebrides.

Dr Blaikie states that the party consisted of the

prince, Donald MacLeod, O'Sullivan, O'Neil, Allan MacDonald, Edward Burke and seven boatmen. This was a mistaken policy, as it proved, for at the very time that the unhappy prince was dodging about the Outer Hebrides avoiding English war vessels the sole object of which was his capture, two French ships arrived in Loch nan Uamh on 3 May and landed a treasure of forty thousand louis d'or under the very guns of three English men-o'-war – the *Greyhound*, *Baltimore* and *Terror*. Many of the prince's council sailed to France in these two ships, including the Duke of Perth, Lord Elcho, Hay and others; the Duke of Perth died on the voyage.

Lochiel, gallant as ever in spite of his wounds, refused to flee, and Murray of Broughton stayed behind with the French treasure and buried it on the shores of Loch Arkaig.

Meanwhile the brutal Cumberland was devastating the Highlands. Every house was burned and nothing was left upon which the unfortunate Highlanders could depend for sustenance. The orders were to annihilate all shelter and all sources of food and to flog any natives from whom information could be obtained by so doing – despite the fact that few of them had any to give.

Cumberland underrated the spirit and traditions of

the Highlands and their people, and although there were traitors among them, such as Murray of Broughton, who turned 'king's evidence' to save his own skin, and Lovat, whose wiles failed to save his head, many of the chiefs were still in possession of their castles and Highland homes. Lochiel held out at Achnacarry; Clanranald in Kinlochmoidart and Cluny Macpherson at Cluny Castle, but not for long, as one by one these strongholds were reduced with a thoroughness that left only smoking ruins and drove the chiefs into the heather.

Cumberland's soldiers burned Achnacarry Castle on 28 May, Kinlochmoidart about the same time and Cluny Castle shortly afterwards.

Interesting stories and traditions of the burning of Cluny Castle have been handed down through the years from generation to generation. On the approach of Cumberland's soldiers on that still cold night in June 1746, when the vigilance in the pursuit of the prince – now known to be in the Hebrides – had relaxed somewhat and, lacking the prince himself, when the vengeance of his victor was directed against his principal supporters, Cluny and his wife fled across the Spey to Breakachy, opposite the castle. Here Cluny climbed a tree near Cat Lodge and watched the search and destruction of his house. Cat

Lodge later became a shooting lodge on the Cluny estate and was originally so named from the crest of Clan Chattan, a wildcat rampant, which bears the interesting motto, 'Touch not the Cat bot a Glove' – one of the few present-day survivals of the old English word 'bot' for 'without', now corrupted into 'but'. This crest and motto were seen on a small standard that was traditionally carried by Clan Chattan at the Battle of Bannockburn.

While her husband watched his burning stronghold, Lady Cluny – to give her the courtesy title invariably accorded to the wives of territorial chieftains in the eighteenth century – sat weeping in the heather on the hillside at Breakachy as the flames devoured the home she loved so well until eventually she found refuge in a corn kiln on the estate and there became the mother of a son, to be afterwards known as 'Duncan of the Kiln'.

It is said that the plantation above Cat Lodge was made to commemorate the sad vigil of Cluny and his wife and that she expressed a wish to be buried among the ruins of her home. All too soon her wish was carried out in the immediate vicinity of the old house, but no one now knows the exact spot. Meanwhile her gallant husband – his self-imposed task of securing the safety of his prince successfully accom-

137

plished – became a hunted fugitive for nine long years, during which time he knew no home but the hills and glens of his wasted countryside and dared stay scarcely more than a single night in one spot for fear of capture. Nevertheless he was saved by the loyalty of his clansmen until at long last he was able to make his escape to France, only to die within a short twelve months – one more of the many thousands who had sacrificed their all to the Stuart claims on their loyalty and to the Stuart charm.

A letter from the Earl Marischal to Cluny congratulating him on his escape still exists:

'NEUFCHATEL, *Jan. 29 1756.*
'SIR – I have the honor of yours and am glad you are safe after escaping many hard pursuits in so long a time as you remained hiding.

'I wish you all happiness wherever you may be taking a real concern in what regards you and your clan as being of the same origine if old tradition does not fail, having ever a warm heart towards you and them and having the honour to be with great regard

'Sir, your most humble and most obedient servant,
MARISCHAL.

Another tale was told at Cluny that Ewan Mac-Pherson (Cluny of the '45), while in hiding, visited his ruined home and there was informed that the English general Sir Hector Munro and a party of Hanoverian soldiers who were searching for the fugitive chieftain were approaching. Hastily stripping himself of all evidence of his rank and clad only in a ragged MacPherson kilt and his shirt, Cluny received his enemy under his own ruined porch and answered the following three questions with a monosyllabic 'No!'

'Is Cluny about?'

'Do you know where he is?'

'Would you tell me if you did know?'

The English officer was so impressed with the supposed clansman's loyalty to his chief that he is stated to have rewarded him with a shilling before resuming his search with the remark that he was 'an honest fellow'. There is a chivalrous doubt implied in the tradition as to whether the general – to whom Cluny's features were probably well known – was not aware of the identity of the 'clansman' but preferred to remain in apparent ignorance of it rather than to enforce his brutal orders for extermination.

The incident is commemorated in a massive piece of plate presented by the clan to Ewan Macpherson of Cluny, the father of a later chieftain and son of Duncan of the Kiln', on his silver wedding. It depicts the Hanoverian general handing the coin to a very defiant Highlander in the person of Ewan Mac-Pherson of the '45.

To return to the prince himself, the inhospitable shores of the mainland had hardly been left behind for the still less hospitable Hebridean seas when the little vessel was overtaken by a storm between the islands of Skye and Rum and was driven to Benbecula, a small island between North and South Uist. Here they hid in a deserted hut for two days while Charles suffered from dysentery, the prince sleeping on a boat sail laid on the bare ground. They killed a cow and boiled the meat in a pot in which they had made their porridge. Charles acted as cook and made a cake of the cow's brains, which they ate sitting on the ground with a rough stone for a table, and the prince is stated to have been in high good humour, which won the hearts of his fellow adventurers.

They then headed for Stornaway on the island of Lewis, arriving at Scalpay Island on 30 April, where the prince remained for several days while Donald MacLeod went on to Stornaway in an endeavour to find a vessel, which he did. The prince then landed on Lewis, at the head of Loch Seaforth, and walked twelve miles across country towards Stornaway, but hearing of his approach the inhabitants of that town refused to allow him to enter it or to have the vessel, and he was obliged to re-embark in the small boat at Arnish for a return to Scalpay. They were chased by ships of war and landed on an uninhabited island, where they remained hidden 'in a low pitiful hut' with a boat sail spread over the roof to keep out the rain. The prince appears to have been enjoying his adventures in spite of the discomforts and was in high spirits.

They reached Scalpay again on 10 May but were again pursued by a ship of war and had to row into shallow water where the warship's deeper draft would not allow her to follow in order to escape. Again they were pursued in Loch Maddy and spent the night at sea. It is recorded that the prince ate heartily of a horrible mixture of oatmeal and sea water, which they called in the Gaelic *stappach*, and that 'never any meat or drink came wrong with him, for he could take his share of everything, good, bad, or indifferent, and was always cheerful and contented in any condition'.

They landed eventually on an island in Loch Uiskevagh and obtained accommodation in a grass-keeper's hut, where they feasted on crabs. Here they stayed for several nights.

A large squadron of ships was now scouring the

Outer Hebridean seas and islands, and the fugitives remained in Glen Corodale in South Uist, in a forester's cottage, for many days until it was apparent that they were being hemmed in.

The prince enjoyed some sport in Corodale and astonished his Highlanders by the skill with which he brought down grouse upon the wing. Here, too, we have the first definite report of the failing that was to prove his ruin in later life. Brandy was plentiful, and O'Neil also says that 'he got the better of us' in more than one protracted carouse with the native MacDonalds of South Uist with whom they fraternized. Neil McEachain also describes the scene after one of these occasions:

'Boystile [MacDonald of Boisdale] came next day and . . . found some of the gentlemen of the country lying in their bed, very much disordered by the foregoing night's carouse, while His Royal Highness was the only one who was able to take care of the rest in heaping them with plaids, and at the same time merrily sang the De Profundis for the repose of their souls.'

Nights were spent in all sorts of rude hiding places, which were graphically described by Hugh MacDonald of Balshar, who visited and caroused with the prince in Corodale, in a letter to Bishop Forbes dated 3 March 1748. The following extracts are taken from Balshar's personal narrative:

'O'Sullivan introduced me to the hutt. He [the prince] saluted me very kindly and told me he was heartily glade to see the face of an honest man in such a remote corner. His dress was then a tartan short coat and vest of the same, got from Lady Clanranald, his nightcap and linen all patched with suit [soot] drops, hands and face patched with the same, a short kilt, tartan hose and Highland brogs, his upper coat being English cloath. He calld a dram being the first article of a Highland Entertainment, which being over he calld for meat . . .

'I spok to Boystill [Boisdale] anent leaving Glencoridile as our stay there woud be of dangerous consequence and of no advantage to him. The young gentleman told us it was but seldom he met with friends he coud enjoy himself with and woud not on any account part with us that night . . .

'The young gentleman advised Edmond Burk, now chairman in Edinburgh, to fill the boul . . .

'Then we began with our boul frank and free, as wee were turning merry wee were turning more free. At last I starts the question if his highness woud take it amiss if I shoud tell him the greatest objections against him in Great Britain. He said not. I told him

143

Popery and arbitrary government were the chiefest. He said it was only bad constructions his enemys put on't. "Do you 'no, Mr M'Donald," he says, "what religion are all the Princes in Europe of?" I told him I imagined they were of the same established religion of the nation they lived in. He told me they had little or no religion at all. Boystill then told him that his predecessor Donald Clanranald had fought seven sett battles for him after the restauration yet he was not ound by King Charles at Court. The Prince said "Boystill, don't be rubbing up old sores, for if I cam home the case woud be otherwise with me." I then says to him that notwithstanding of what freedom wee enjoyed there with him wee coud've no access to him if he was setled at London; he told us then if we had never so much ado, he'd be one night merry with his Highland friends. Wee continued this drinking for 3 days and 3 nights. He still had the better of us and even of Boystill himself notwithstanding his being as able a boulman, I dare say, as any in Scotland.'

The prince's party next was driven farther south to Loch Boisdale near the southern tip of South Uist where they had to conceal themselves in a creek while fifteen ships of war and a number of soldiers were searching for them. Several nights were spent in the open fields, sheltered under their boat sail, until on 21 June Charles was guided by Neil McEachair (in English 'son of Hector') to a hut near Ormacleit at midnight, where for the first time the prince met his gallant and romantic preserver, Flora Macdonald, whose assistance was asked in order that he might be taken to the island of Skye.

Before parting with Donald MacLeod and his boatmen the prince paid each man a shilling a day out of his little store and gave a draft to Donald Mac-Leod for sixty pistoles to be paid by his secretary, John Hay of Restalrig, when Donald should meet him. Bishop Forbes remarks, 'but as Donald never met with Mr Hay the draught remains yet unpaid', and that Donald wept at the woeful parting but in-sisted that he hoped to see the prince again and did not despair of payment of his 'draught' with interest, 'old as he was'.

Donald added that the prince 'used to smoak a great deal of tobacco', but as his pipes broke he turned them into short cutties and, taking quills, fit-ted one into the other and all into the end of the cutty 'to make it long enough and the tobacco to smoak cool'.

Donald was captured shortly after parting from the prince and spent a year in confinement, first as a prisoner on board the *Furnace* under the egregious Captain Ferguson and afterwards in London, suffering great hardships and cruelties at the hands of his captors. He was taken before General Campbell, who questioned him closely and asked if he had been 'along with the Pretender'.

'Yes,' said Donald, 'I was with that young gentleman, and I wunna deny it.'

'Do you know,' asked the General, 'that money was upon that young man's head? No less a sum than *thirty thousand pounds* sterling, which would have made you and all your children after you happy for ever.'

Donald replied, 'What then? Thirty thousand pounds! Though I had gotten it I could not have enjoyed it eight-and-forty hours. Conscience would have gotten up upon me and the money could not have kept it down, and though I could have gotten all England and Scotland for my pains I would not have allowed a hair of his body to be touched if I could help it.'

What loyalty! what disinterested self-sacrifice!

The general was forced to reply: 'I will not say you are in the wrong, but now you are in the King's mercy, and if you will not declare everything you know of this matter, here is a machine that will force you to declare,' pointing to Boisdale's rack on which he would torture supposed thieves on the Isle of

Skye to force them to confess. Donald's naive reply was to the effect that it could now do no harm, as the prince had escaped to the mountains and that he would tell all he knew without the help of 'any machine whatever'.

Donald and Malcolm MacLeod, who was also a prisoner with many others, including 'sixty or seventy of the Grants of Glen Moriston' who had surrendered at Inverness at the request of the chief, Ludovic Grant, under promise of pardon, were treated with repulsive cruelty, and it is stated by them in their accounts that four hundred Highlanders died on board three ships opposite Tilbury Fort in the Thames. They declared that no finer or stouter men ever drew sword than were these men of Glen Moriston, but all died 'save one or two' who survived to return to their native glen and that the treatment of the Grants by their chief, 'who hated the Glenmoriston men' and who induced them to surrender, was a warning to others not to follow their example. They were fed on horse flesh and putrid meat, and all on the ship were sick and dying – they were allowed no fresh or clean clothes but were covered by verminous rags until at last Donald was released on 10 June 1747, and on 17 August following he gave his attested account to Bishop Forbes. He

147

was presented with a very ornate snuffbox by a Jacobite admirer before he left London, and on showing it to Bishop Forbes the latter asked him why there was no snuff in it. His reply is a charming example of his native simplicity: 'Sneeshin in that box? Na! Na! the deel a pickle sneeshin shall ever go into it till the King be restored, and then, I trust in God, I'll go to London, and then will I put sneeshin in the box and go to the Prince and say, "Sir, will you tak' a sneeshin oot o' my box?"'

To return to Prince Charles and Flora Macdonald, it should be stated that the many romantic but otherwise mistaken tales of any relationship between Charles Edward and Flora, or any suggestion that she was ever his mistress, are absolutely without foundation. Flora was a young, generous, high-spirited, self-sacrificing Highland woman whose sole desire was to serve her prince in his hour of need, and that she was always treated and remembered with the utmost reverence and gratitude by the royal fugitive is beyond doubt.

On 22 June the prince spent the night under a rock while Flora and Neil McEachain were cross-examined as to his whereabouts by a militia guard but were not detained. On 23 June they had to return to the little island of Wiay, and rowed the following morning to Benbecula, reaching Rossinish late at night, which they spent in the house of a tenant of Clanranald's. They had to flee the following day to avoid a militia search and spent the day in the open in the pouring rain, returning to the hut when the militia had gone. Here, on the 27th, they were joined by Lady Clanranald and her daughter and by Flora MacDonald, but during supper – which consisted of kidneys broiled on a spit by the royal 'chef', who placed Flora on his right hand with Lady Clanranald on his left and they 'all dined very heartily' – they heard that General Campbell with a large force was closing in on them.

On the 28th Lady Clanranald was summoned to attend General Campbell, and with her husband was shortly afterwards taken prisoner.

On the same evening Flora MacDonald provided the prince with female clothing 'of a gown of light sprigged calico, a petticoat, a mantle of dun camlet, with a hood to cover the head in the Irish fashion', and Charles, acting as her maid, 'Betty Burke', they embarked on a boat and sailed for the island of Skye. On the voyage the prince sang several songs and is said to have sung Flora to sleep.

On the 29th, on their arrival at Waternish Point in Skye, they found it occupied by troops who fired at them, and they were obliged to row off from the point and land at Mongestot,[1] where Flora, having first been questioned by a militia officer as to who she was, induced Lady Margaret MacDonald to send refreshments to the prince, who walked seven miles to Kingsburgh House and spent the night there.

MacDonald of Kingsburgh and his wife gave personal testimonies to the prince's cheerful disposition in their account of this visit. Thus Mrs MacDonald states that she employed her daughter as handmaid to the prince in putting on his woman's dress on rising the next morning, 'for de'el a preen could he put in it. When Miss MacDonald was a-dressing of him he was like to fall over a-laughing, and after the peeness, gown, hood, mantle, etc, had been put on he said, "O Miss, you have forgot my apron. Where is my apron? Pray get me my apron here, for that is the principal part of my dress."'

Kingsburgh and his wife both declared that the prince behaved not like anyone who was in danger but as cheerfully as if he had been putting on women's clothes merely for the amusement of others.

---

[1] The spelling of these places on the prince's route varies considerably in different, and even in the same, accounts. Thus Mongestot is spelled 'Mougstot' and 'Monkstat' by Dr Blaikie and 'Mugstot' by Andrew Lang.

On the evening of 30 June:

'Kingsburgh was at pains to represent to the prince the inconveniency and danger of his being in a female dress, particularly from his airs being all so man-like, and told him that he was very bad at acting the part of a dissembler. He advised him therefore to take from him a suit of Highland cloaths with a broad-sword in his hand, which would become him much better. But in the meantime that he should go out of his house in the female dress, lest the servants should be making their observations, and stop at the edge of a wood upon the side of a hill, not far from the house, where he and others should come to him with the Highland cloaths, broadsword, etc.'

Many of Neil McEachain's descriptions of the prince's moods and manners are greatly diverting, as, for instance, on a Sunday when he heard the country people discussing the strange behaviour of the supposed serving maid, who insisted on walking with Kingsburgh and speaking to him in familiar terms. The local prudes cursed her for the terrible steps that she took and the careless manner in which she carried her dress. But the climax came when they arrived at a knee-deep rivulet and had to cross it, 'to see Burke take up her pettycoat so high when she entered the water the poor fellows were quite confounded at this last sight'.

At Kingsburgh House we hear of another gathering and the prince's desire to make a night of it, but he was at last induced by his faithful host to go to bed, and he slept nine hours. In the morning Mrs MacDonald took Flora to his room to beg for a lock of his hair, which she cut while he laid his head upon her lap. Part of this lock was set in a ring, said to be the prince's parting gift.

The prince changed his female clothes for the Highland costume, as advised by Kingsburgh, and walked to Portree with Neil McEachain, Flora meanwhile riding near them by the main road to signal any approach of danger.

Kingsburgh was arrested a few days later (probably 4 July) as a result of threats to the prince's boatmen, who had brought him and Flora from Uist and who were captured on their return and threatened with torture and death if they refused to tell where they had landed him.

On extracting the necessary information, Captain John Ferguson, a notoriously brutal officer, was dispatched by General Campbell to proceed to Sir Alexander MacDonald's house at Mongestot and to trace and arrest the fugitives. He searched Mongestot and also Kingsburgh before arresting the laird, and his examination of Mrs MacDonald and her daughter is narrated by Bishop Forbes:

'Kingsburgh told his lady that Captain Ferguson was come to ask about some lodgers she had lately in her house, and desired her to be distinct in her answers. Mrs MacDonald, looking Ferguson broad in the face, said, "If Captain Ferguson is to be my judge, then God have mercy upon my soul!" Ferguson asked for what reason she spoke such words. "Why, Sir," said she, "the world belies you if you be not a very cruel, hard-hearted man; and indeed I do not like to come through your hands."'

Ferguson proceeded to question Kingsburgh where Flora 'and the person along with her in woman's cloathes lay all night', and Kingsburgh referred to his wife. Bishop Forbes relates that 'he had the impertinence to ask Mrs MacDonald whether or not she had laid the Young Pretender and Miss MacDonald in one bed?' To which she answered with spirit, 'Sir, whom you mean by the Young Pretender I shall not pretend to guess, but I can assure you it is not the fashion in the Isle of Skye to lay the mistress and the maid in the same bed together.'

Ferguson insisted on seeing the different rooms in

which the fugitives slept and commented on the fact that the 'maid' had the better.

After his arrest Kingsburgh was taken before General Campbell and admitted harbouring the escaped prince. He was released exactly twelve months later, 4 July 1747, and on 11 July in that year, while a guest at the house of Lady Bruce of Kinross in the citadel of Leith, he not only gave a full and succinct account of the incident of the prince's visit in the presence of fourteen or fifteen people but corrected many local place names and distances in the narratives previously given by MacKinnon, Malcolm MacLeod and Flora MacDonald herself, which had been compiled into journal form by Bishop Forbes.

The incident of the gift to Flora of a lock of hair is interesting and such definite proof of the prince's chivalry and consideration for the woman who preserved his life that it may well be repeated from Bishop Forbes's account:

'After Miss Flora had got up, Mrs MacDonald told her that she wanted much to have a lock of the Prince's hair, and that she behoved to go into his room and get it for her. Miss Flora refused, as the Prince was not yet out of bed. "What then," said Mrs MacDonald, "no harm will happen to you; he is too good to harm you or any person, you must instantly

go and get me the lock!" Mrs MacDonald taking
hold of Miss with one hand knocked at the door. The
Prince called, "Who is there?" Mrs MacDonald
opening the door said, "Sir, it is I, and I am impor-
tuneing Miss Flora to come in and get a lock of your
hair for me and she refuses to do it." "Pray," said the
Prince, "desire Miss MacDonald to come in. What
should make her afraid to come where I am?" When
Miss came in he begged her to sit in a chair by the
bedside, then laying his arms about her waist and his
head upon her lap he desired her to cut out the lock
with her own hands in token of future and more sub-
stantial favours. The one half of the lock Miss gave to
Mrs MacDonald, and the other she kept for herself. I
have heard Mrs MacDonald say that when Flora at
any time happened to come into the room where the
Prince was, he always rose from his seat, paid her the
same respect as if she had been a queen, and made her
sit on his right hand.'

An empty enough reward for one who had done so
much for him – perhaps – but at least the highest
honour that could be paid her by a hunted fugitive.

Flora MacDonald married Allan, the son of this
same Mrs MacDonald and of the prince's other preserver, Alexander MacDonald of Kingsburgh, at Ar-
nadale in Skye on 6 November 1750. They lived in
their own house until the death of old Kingsburgh in

155

1766 and then moved to the ancestral home. In 1775 they emigrated to North Carolina but were driven back to Skye by the insurrection in North America, and Flora died at Kingsburgh on 5 March 1790. Her grave is in a romantic situation, close to the spot where she made her memorable landing with Prince Charles in 1746.

At Portree Flora took her leave of the prince, whose final words were: 'I hope we shall meet in St James's yet, and I will reward you there for what you have done.'

She was arrested a week afterwards, after Charles, with three of the MacLeods, had crossed to the island of Raasay, but he considered his new hiding unsafe and returned to Skye the same evening, spending the night in a cow byre near Nicholson's Rock. Here he parted from his attendants, except Malcolm MacLeod, whose servant he pretended to be, and walked all night to Elgol, a distance of nearly twenty miles, where he met MacKinnon and left the same evening (4 July) with the old chieftain and other members of the clan for the mainland, landing on the shores of Loch Nevis and spending three or four nights on the open moor. They then crossed to Knoydart, after being chased by some of the militia, and here met old Clanranald who, however, refused them assistance, so that they returned to Mallaig and from there walked at night to Morar, where, the chief's house having been burned, he was living in a hut.

Charles and his little party hid in a cave and from there arrived in Borradale on the morning of 10 July, the very spot from which he had sailed three months earlier and at which he had landed on 25 July in the previous year. What memories his return there must have evoked.

Here the MacKinnons left him and, as appeared to be the case with all his helpers, both were arrested the following day. This led to the prince moving four miles to the east, where he stayed in 'MacLeod's Cave', which is supposed to have been situated on a high precipice in the woods of Borradale. He was now under the protection of the MacDonalds, and John MacDonald, Borradale's son, is said to have seen that the whole coast was surrounded by ships of war and the country by military forces. The prince therefore moved farther to the east and rested in Beinn nan Cabar, but with General Campbell and a large force in the neighbourhood, and hearing that Clanranald's lands were entirely surrounded by troops from the head of Loch Eil to Loch Hourn, it was evident that news of his landing had leaked out and that if he was to avoid capture he must break through the line of sentries.

All through the night of 18 July they walked through the Braes of Morar, and on the 20th, on approaching the top of Druimachosi, they learned that troops were marching up the other side of the hill, and from the summit they observed that they were close up to the enemy's camp. On the 21st they passed through the line of guards, and it is said that here Charles narrowly escaped falling over a precipice but managed to save himself by clutching a tree. They lay on the moor, concealed by the long heather and branches of young birch bushes, and the next day came to Glen Shiel. Here it was that Charles made up his mind to go to the wilds of Glen Moriston, and early on the morning of the 23rd arrived at Strath Cluny, wet to the skin. They spent the night in an open cave, and the following morning met the faithful 'eight men of Glen Moriston' who conducted Charles to the Coiraghoth Cave, where he is said to have been 'as comfortably lodged as if in a royal palace'. Here he remained for a week, but troops were again closing in so the party struck north to avoid them, again finding shelter in Strath Glass in a shieling, and stayed in this neighbourhood for a further week, when they heard that a French ship had landed two officers to search for the prince in Lochiel's country.

On 12 August they again reached the Braes of Glen Moriston and found that the English troops were abandoning the search and that the road to Glen Garry was now clear. The weather had broken – it was raining persistently, but the prince, in high spirits, passed through Glen Loyne and forded the River Garry in high spate with much difficulty, spending the night on the side of a hill above the stream, exposed to the elements and wet to the skin. They were entirely without food when one of the Glen Moriston men had the good fortune to shoot a fine stag and so relieved their hunger.

Travelling on to the side of Loch Arkaig they were joined by several other fugitives, and on the 17th a message was sent to find and bring Lochiel to the prince. On the 20th Dr Archie Cameron arrived with a message that Lochiel was too badly hurt to be able to come himself and to make his excuses. Here too they fell in with the two French officers and until the 27th were in constant danger. Grant of Knockandhu discovered their hiding place, and frequent changes of sleeping quarters in neighbouring glens and straths were necessary before Archie Cameron returned from Lochiel with a message to the prince

159

to join him and Cluny MacPherson in the latter's 'fast place' on Ben Alder's side.

The prince's appearance at this period of his 'skulking' was graphically portrayed by John Cameron, Presbyterian minister and chaplain at Fort William, who was with Dr Cameron at the time:

'The Prince had gone a little from the hutt, but being informed what we were came immediately to us. He was then bare-footed, had an old black kilt coat on, a plaid, philabeg and waistcoat, a dirty shirt and a long red beard, a gun in his hand, a pistol and dirk by his side. He was very cheerful and in good health, and, in my opinion, fatter than when he was at Inverness.'

The devoted 'eight men of Glen Moriston' were dismissed, and on 28 August their gallant leader, Patrick Grant, took his final leave of his prince, who gave him twenty-four guineas to divide with his seven friends.

On 30 August he at last met Lochiel, whom he had not seen since they parted at Culloden Moor, four and a half months previously. With Lochiel were MacPherson of Breakachy, a brother-in-law of Cluny, Allan Cameron and two of Cluny's servants and clansmen. The gallant old chieftain of Clan Cameron was still suffering badly from his wound and was hid-

ing in a little shieling on Mellaneuir, or Mealan Od-
har, a hill in Ben Alder forest. Lochiel at first mistook
the prince's party for enemies, and they were covered
with a dozen muskets before the chieftain recognized
the prince and hobbled forward to pay the usual
homage. Charles insisted that he should not kneel to
him, and the two parties joined forces, moving on to
another shieling farther into the forest 'superlatively
bad and smockie' after Cluny MacPherson joined
them on 2 September. On the 5th they moved to
'Cluny's Cage' at the side of Loch Ericht, on the face
of a rough slope of grey stone on the steep side of
Ben Alder, where it frowns over the waters of Loch
Ericht at the western end and overlooking Rannoch
Moor and Schiehallion in the distance.

Dr Blaikie says that the actual site of the cage is not
quite certain, 'though tradition has grown up round
a cave above Ben Alder Lodge near the southwestern
end of Loch Ericht'. This cave has since fallen in, but
there is no doubt locally that this was indeed the
home of the prince for over a week and it was well
situated for concealment.

The only romantic description of the site is an exact picture of the scene, believed to have been written
from Cluny's own description, as reproduced by Dr
Blaikie:

'About five miles to the south westward of his Chateau [Cluny Castle], commenced his forrest of Ben Alder, plentifully stocked with dear, red hares, moorfoul, and other game of all kinds, besides which it affords fine pasture for his numberous flocks and heards. There also he keeps a harras of some hundred mares, all which after the fatal day of Culoden became the pray of his enemies. It contains an extent of many mountains and small valleys, in all computed about twelve miles long East and West, and from eight to ten miles in breadth, without a single house in the whole except the necessary lodges for the shepherds who were charged with his flocks. It was in this forrest where the prince found Cluny with Lochiell in his wounds and other friends under his care. He was afraid that his constitution might not suit with lying on the ground or in caves, so was solicitous to contrive a more comfortable habitation for him upon the south front of one of these mountains, overlooking a beautiful lake of twelve miles long.[1] He observed a thicket of hollywood, he went, viewed and found it fit for his purpose; he cause immediately wave the thicket round with boughs, made a first and second floor in it, and covered it with moss to defend the rain. The uper room servd for salle à manger and

---

[1] Cluny was out in his estimation here, by English measurement, as Loch Ericht is full fifteen miles long, and the site of the cage is about two miles from its southwestern end on the western slope of Ben Alder.

bed chamber, while the lower servd for a cave to contain liquors and other necessaries, at the back part was a proper hearth for cook and baiker, and the face of the mountain had so much the colour and resemblance of smock, no person coud ever discover that there was either fire or habitation in the place. Round this lodge were placed sentinels at proper stations, some nearer and some at greater distances, who dayly brought them notice of what happened in the country, and even in the enemies camps, bringing them likewise the necessary provisions, while a neighbouring fountain supplied the society with the rural refreshment of pure rock water. As, therefore, an oak tree is to this day reverd in Brittain for having happily savd the great Uncle Charles the Second, from the pursuits of Cromwell, so this holly thicket will probablie in future times be likewise reverd for having savd Prince Charles, the nephew, from the still more dangerous pursuits of Cumberland, who showed himself on all occasions a much more inveterate enemy. In this romantick humble habitation the Prince dwelt, when news of the ships being arrived reached him, Cluny conveyed him to them with joy, happy in having so safely placd so valuable a charge, then returned with contentment, alone to commence his pilgrimage, which continued for nine years more. And now notwithstanding the very great difference of his present situation and circumstances to what

they once were, he is always gay and cheerful, conscious of having done his duty, he defys fortune to
make him express his mind unhappy, or so much as
make him think of any action below his honour.'

Well may Andrew Lang write of the gallant and
self-sacrificing chieftain who gave his all in his
prince's service:

'At home in a hundred dangers, preserved only by
the inviolable and sleepless vigilance of the children
of his tribe, remained Cluny; himself (if the ancient
laws of Celtic hereditary custom had existed) the Le-
gitimist King of Scotland, the representative through
the house of MacHeth, of the blood of Lulach. After
an Odyssey of adventures the house of Lochiel still
retains the old lands, and the affection and respect of
Highlands and Lowlands; while, at the close of services even more arduous Clan Vourich yet boasts a
Cluny to represent that Celtic royal line, compared
with which the Stuarts were parvenus and interlop-
ers.'

But what of the last of those Stuarts? After eight
days in 'Cluny's Cage' with his companions, one of
the MacPhersons arrived with news that two French
vessels had arrived in Loch nan Uamh, and on 13
September the party started for the coast. Travelling

always at night and 'keeping themselves private by day', they reached Borradale on 19 September and embarked on one of the two French vessels, probably the *Prince of Conti* – the other being *L'Heureux* – under the care of Colonel Warren, who reported on l0 October to the Chevalier that 'this moment at half-past two in the afternoon' he had 'happily arrived within four leagues of Morlaix'.

Even at the very last the prince did not forget those who had served him, as has so often been alleged against him, for a document, still preserved, is addressed to 'MacPherson of Cluny':

'Diralagich in Glencamagier of Locharkag, 18th of Septr. 1746.

'As we are sensible of your and clans fidelity and integrity to us dureing our adventures in Scotland and England in the year 1745–1746 in recovering our just rights from the Elector of Hanover by which interest you have sustained very great losses both in your interest and person I therefore promise when it shall please God to put it in my power to make a greatfull return sutable to your sufferings.

Charles P. R.'

Every account of Charles's behaviour during his lurking in the heather records him as carefree and

165

happy, and his courage and endurance as being beyond praise. Lochgarry, writing to Glengarry of the journey to join Lochiel and Cluny, says:

'We travelld three days and nights without much eating or any sleep but slumbering now and then on a hillside. Our indefatigable Prince bore this with greater courage and resolution than any of us, nor never was there a Highlander born coud travel up and down hills better or suffer more fatigues. Show me a King or Prince in Europe coud have borne the like or a tenth of it.'

The same writer says that they had 'one hundred miles to travell to where the ships were', but if we put it at eighty-five English miles, which is more like the actual distance covered, and realize that they traversed this distance over almost trackless mountains and valleys and reached the French vessels in six nights, we may well marvel with Lochgarry at the courage and endurance of this last of the royal Stuarts and pay him that measure of admiration which his gallant conduct deserves.

Sir Robert Strange was also in hiding 'in the heather' for several weeks, and otherwise once escaped by creeping under the ample hooped petticoat of his 'lady love', Isabella Lumisden, as she was singing at her work, while soldiers were searching the house for the fugitive.

He eventually reached Edinburgh, where, still in hiding, he supported himself by painting portraits of the various leaders on both sides in the recent rebellion, which he sold at a guinea each. He obtained a safe-conduct to London, and with others not specially included in the Act of Attainder or exempted from the Act of Grace in June 1747, he received a free pardon, married his constant lady love, Isabella, in the same year and subsequently, after first refusing to do so in 1775, acted as portrait painter to the court in London and was knighted by King George III in 1787 for his pictures of two of the royal children who had recently died.

CHAPTER VI

FINAL SHADOWS

The story of the prince's adventure draws to a close, and with it the shadowy passage of the kings and princes of Scotland's royal Stuart line across the stage of British history. For upwards of four hundred and fifty years, it provided stories of romance, intrigue and character that contributed to the final curtain. If only it were possible to have recorded the end of 'Bonnie Prince Charlie' in some final action in the country for which he had fought and striven so gallantly or in some storm at sea that would have left his honour unsullied and his memory untarnished. Then, indeed, he would have gone down in history as a 'very perfect knight', whom Scotland and England could alike revere without reservation.

Andrew Lang expresses a similar sentiment in his account of the Battle of Culloden: 'All the world has regretted that the prince did not fall, as Keppoch fell, leaving an unblemished record behind him', but that gifted writer would thus have robbed his hero of his greatest romance, when, to use his own words, he was 'skulking in the heather', when for six long months the whole might of England was aimed at the capture of one poor fugitive who had only his own wits and those of a handful of devoted followers to rely upon to save him from discovery and death. Andrew Lang would have robbed Flora Macdonald of her immortality and the prince's preservers, the Glen Moriston men, Lochiel, Cluny, Neil McEach-ain and the other gallant spirits of the Highlands and Islands, of their undying fame.

Without those six months of peril and hardship so gallantly borne, the epic story of Prince Charles Edward Stuart would have been shorn of half its appeal to sympathy and imagination. What remains to be told can only evoke feelings of sorrow and perhaps pity.

On his arrival in France, Prince Charles's first action was to write to his brother, the Duke of York, that he must see the French king as soon as possible, and he went to Paris for that purpose. But the young adventurer found, as all must in such cases, that the failure of his attempt had placed him in a very different position from that which he had occupied before it was made. Then he was a power to be considered and dreaded by the English government, a personality to be reckoned with; now he had returned a hunted fugitive, his followers dispersed or dead, and brilliant as his attempt had been, greatly as he had enhanced his personal fame, applauded as he was by the people, he had returned with 'failure' written boldly across his page of history.

Louis XV, therefore, declined to recognize Charles in public, and although he was received in private at Versailles and appears to have been well and even affectionately treated, it was more as the 'friend and cousin' than as a prince of England.

Charles did his best to counteract this by public appearances at the opera and elsewhere, glittering with his orders and jewels, and was received with acclaim on account of his romantic adventure. This unfortunately created something like jealousy in the breast of the religious and narrower mind of his brother, who fancied himself slighted and avoided by the elder's associates and brothers-in-arms, while the prince cordially detested the scheming priests and others who were in his brother's confidence. Charles, in October, wrote of this to the king of France and bluntly stated, 'The reason why I did not speak to Your Majesty about my affairs last night was because my brother was present, and loving him tenderly, I was anxious to avoid giving him cause for jealousy.'

So matters drifted on. King Louis made adequate and even generous provision for the maintenance of the two princes Paris, but Charles would have none of it and bluntly told the king that he would leave Paris and so avoid raising false hopes in the minds of his friends and supporters rather than accept a pension, which involved abandoning his hopes of immediate military and monetary assistance to repeat the attempt that had so nearly succeeded.

Over and over again for nearly two years the prince himself, his father from Rome and that most gallant and steadfast supporter of the exiled house, Cameron of Lochiel, entreated the French king for assistance, for those 'succours' so often promised but not fully delivered – if it were not indeed the French policy rather to keep alive the prospect of a Jacobite invasion, and so continually to play upon the minds and fears of the English ministers, than to remove them by a Jacobite restoration and run the risk of strengthening the British arms against France by having a united people in the island kingdom under a Jacobite king when next one of the inevitable wars between the two countries was imminent.

For some time, too, marriage projects for both princes were constantly proposed and considered by the Chevalier and his advisers but came to nothing.

Charles left Paris early in 1747, writing to his father from Lyons and from Avignon, and even went to Spain but there received a cold welcome and little encouragement. Eventually he was given an interview by the king but only to be urged to leave Spanish territory for fear of complications. Here we have the first hint of actual drunkenness in the prince and of his frequenting the company of his confessor, Father Kelly, who had the reputation of being a confirmed drunkard.

Charles was obliged to return to Paris in March 1747. Meanwhile the dissensions between the two brothers had become more acute, and the unfortunate Chevalier was the recipient of complaints from each about the conduct of the other.

The prince, not without reason when we remember the insolent letter that had been written after Culloden, behaved in a very cavalier manner to Lord George Murray, who visited him in Paris, and Charles received a very severe letter from his father for his treatment of his one-time general, James describing it as 'unchristian, unprincely, and impolite'.

Early in 1747, too, we see the first of the Duke of

York's intention to enter the priesthood, and while Charles was in Spain Henry wrote to the Chevalier expressing his abhorrence at the idea of marrying and telling his father of his desire and vocation, and in April he received his father's blessing and approval of the project. The Duke of York seems to have acted with singular and unusual duplicity. He asked Charles to a banquet and made extraordinary preparations in his honour, but when the guest arrived he found the host missing and merely received a letter, which Lang says was not delivered until three days later, telling him that Henry must see his father if only for a few days, bidding him farewell and regretting his leaving without telling his brother of his intentions.

Charles realized that this meant the end of all their hopes, and he was, not unnaturally, furious when he received his father's information that the duke would soon be made a cardinal. The news caused the utmost consternation, and the step was considered a worse blow to Jacobite aspirations even than the Battle of Culloden.

Charles wrote to his father that though 'I cannot help loving him it will be impossible for me now to have any commerce with him', and he kept to his word for nearly twenty years. He believed, not without reason, that England's influence with Cardinal Tencin had been used to secure a step so fatal to the Stuart cause. Long periods of silence ensued, alternating with others during which the prince's letters became shorter and shorter and his movements vague and uncertain.

Matters drifted on until the Treaty of Aix-la-Chapelle was imminent, and the prince, as regent of Great Britain, sent a protest against the usurpation of his father's kingdom by the 'Elector of Hanover', but the final signing of the treaty made his presence in Paris no longer possible, and the French government sent him formal notification that he must quit Paris and leave French territory.

The unhappy prince was now hurrying down the abyss that had opened at his feet and was only too readily the prey of wild companions and the vice that he had indulged in on occasion in Scotland. It is said that at this period, too, he amused himself with many illicit love affairs, and he certainly lived with Princess de Talmond for a time.

Instead, therefore, of quietly leaving France, as desired by his father once the terms of the treaty had been finally sealed, he practically defied the French king and government and actually twice wrote his regrets at being obliged to disobey the king's request.

The French king appealed to the Chevalier, who added his own command to that of the 'most Christian King'. Still Charles refused to quit Paris, and he openly rejoiced in the victories of the English fleet over the French, even going so far as to cause the striking of a medal with his profile bust on the obverse and the British fleet shown on the reverse.

This defiance was too much, and finally, all other projects failing, Charles was arrested on 9 December 1748 at the door of the Opera House in Paris, bound and carried to the Castle of Vincennes. He was, however, released and on 15 December was conducted to the frontier of Savoy. From there he travelled via Lyons to Avignon, where he appeared on the morning of the 27th. Here, however, he offended the papal authorities, and under orders from the pope, who feared French reprisals, he left Avignon on 29 February and disappeared from the eyes of all his friends.

He is known to have again visited Paris, Venice, Lorraine, Poland, Berlin – and certainly London, once, if not twice, in the ensuing five years – but all the records are confused and uncertain, except for a hectic week in London in September 1750, when, with some considerable preparation on the part of his supporters, which took the form of the making

175

of snuffboxes containing his portrait, little tokens with his head in profile, small busts in marble, intaglios and other propaganda for distribution amongst the Stuart supporters, he suddenly appeared at the house of Lady Primrose in Essex Street, Strand, and startled the English Jacobites into some activity.

The Oak Society was in the habit of meeting at the Crown and Anchor Inn in the Strand, opposite the Church of St Clement Danes, and it is probable that Charles attended one or more of their meetings, for special glasses were engraved for that society, bearing the usual Jacobite emblems and the words *Revirescit, Redeat* and other mottoes, and the society even went to the length of striking a special medal, dated 1750, with the prince's portrait by Charles Norbert Roettiers on the obverse and the motto *Revirescit* ('It flourishes anew') above an oak sapling springing from the roots of a decayed oak tree, on the reverse – a significant suggestion of his replacement of his failing father's energies.

Again a similar medal was struck and dated in 1752, bearing the motto *Redeat magnvs ille genius Brittanniae* ('May he, the great genius of Britain, return') around the bust as before, and on the reverse a British ship and a figure of Britannia with the motto *O diu desiderata navis* ('Oh, long-hoped-for ship'), and in the exergue, the space below the design on the reverse of a medal, *Laetamini cives Sept* XXIII MDCCLII ('Let us rejoice, citizens, 23rd Sept. 1752'), which appear to be commemorative of these two visits. It is certain that the first visit took place in September 1750 and that he arrived on the 16th and left again on the 22nd. The second visit was probably in September (?23rd) 1752, and on one of these visits Charles renounced the Roman Catholic religion in the Church of St Mary le Strand. Lang gives the date of this renunciation as 1750, as also does the prince himself in one of his notes, 'To mention my religion of the Church of England as by law established, as I have declared myself when in London, the year 1750,' but the same author says that John Home gives the report that Charles was admitted to the communion of the English Church 'in the New Church in the Strand in 1753' and, further, that the conversion was known to Lord Denbigh and Sir James Harrington in the autumn of 1752. It is possible that the two visits have been confused, that Charles himself – as he frequently did in his later years when his memory was failing – mixed them up and that the conversion actually took place on that 'September 23rd 1752' engraved on the medal. It is asserted that the visit in the latter year was known about and connived at by the British government as a simple means of killing any further hopes of a restoration, and if that were so it accounts for Charles's conversion being known to Denbigh and Harrington in 'the autumn of 1752'. It is quite certain that the fact that Charles was in London was known to Lord Holdernesse, the Secretary of State, and that he reported the fact to George II, who decided to take no action, wisely realizing that the prince would soon be convinced that his opportunity was gone forever.

Probably at the close of the 1750 visit, Clementina Walkinshaw joined him, as her sister was in London in attendance on the Princess of Wales; certainly she was with him shortly afterwards. In many disguises he wandered about the Continent. He is known to have attended a ball at the Opera House in Paris in March 1751, and the English government received a report from their ambassador in Paris that he was travelling through Spain and Italy disguised as a friar.

Clementina was with Charles in the Netherlands in 1752 and at Ghent shortly afterwards, and in this and the succeeding year it is probable that all his plots and many of his movements were communicated to the English government by 'Pickle the Spy', whom Andrew Lang identified in his book of that name as Alastair MacDonnell the Younger of Glengarry. Lang was undoubtedly correct in his revelation of the identity of 'Pickle', and his discovery threw a lurid light upon many mysterious occurrences, for Glengarry was a familiar and frequent correspondent of the prince, and it is now clear that every movement and meeting was reported to the prime minister, Henry Pelham. This traitor, Glengarry, was also primarily responsible for the arrest and execution in 1753 of Dr Archie Cameron, the brother of Lochiel, who assisted in saving the prince from 'Cluny's Cage' on Ben Alder.

Perhaps the best and most disinterested tribute to the character of Prince Charles was written by this same Dr Archibald Cameron in the Tower of London on the night before his execution at Tyburn on 7 June 1753. That a man who had suffered so greatly in the prince's cause, who had lived with him continuously for over two years after his defeat, could so write is surely eloquent testimony to his personal charm and attributes and demands reproduction of his words in full.

'My attachment to the royal family is more the result of examination and conviction than of prepossession and prejudice. And as I am now, so I was then, ready to seal my loyalty with my blood. As soon, therefore, as the royal youth had set up the king his father's standard, I immediately, as in duty bound, repaired to it, and as I had the honour from that time to be almost constantly about his person till November, 1748, excepting the short time after the affair of Culloden that His Royal Highness was in the Western Isles, I became more and more captivated with his amiable and princely virtues which are indeed in every instance so eminently great as I want words to describe. I can further affirm (and my present situation and that of my dear Prince too, can leave no room to suspect me of flattery) that as I have been his companion in the lowest degree of adversity that ever Prince was reduced to, so I have beheld him too, as it were, on the highest pinnacle of glory, amidst the continual applauses and I had almost said adorations of the most brilliant Court in Europe, yet he was always the same, ever affable and courteous, giving constant proof of his great humanity and of his love for his friends and his country. What great good to these nations might not be expected from such a Prince were he in possession of the throne of his ancestors! And as to his courage! None that have ever heard of his glorious attempt in 1745 can, I should think, call it in question.

'I cannot pass by in silence that most unjust and horrid calumny (viz. the giving no quarter to our enemy) raised by the rebels under the command of the inhumann son of the Elector of Hanover which served as an excuse for the *unparallelled butchery* committed by his orders in cold blood after the unhappy affair of Culloden which, if true, must have come to my knowledge who had the honour to serve my ever dear master in quality of one of his Aides-de-Camp. And I hereby declare I never heard of such orders. The above is truth.

'I likewise declare on the word of a dying man that the last time I had the honour to see His Royal Highness Charles Prince of Wales, he told me from his own mouth and bid me assure his friends from him that he was a member of the Church of England.

Archibald Cameron.'

Dr Cameron was the last Jacobite to suffer for his participation in the rebellion of seven years previously, and his death is only one more instance of the implacable hatred and thirst for vengeance on its defeated foes that the English government evinced. He was sentenced to be hanged 'but not until you are dead', with all the revolting cruelties of disembowelling during life and dismemberment after death that were the penalties of treason.

In Paris in the same year Clementina gave birth to a daughter, Charlotte, and shortly afterwards Charles wrote that he was discarding his Catholic servants and that 'my mistress has behaved so unworthily that she has put me out of patience and as she is a Papist too I discard her also'. He was now almost at his lowest point. Driven from country to country, inebriated and selling his clothes and his arms to buy sustenance, he did not, however, 'discard' Clementina and her infant but perhaps sentenced them to a worse fate, for they were destined to follow him in his weary and fruitless wanderings. Spies dogged his footsteps everywhere, and one by one he alienated all his friends. One faithful secretary, Goring, repeatedly offered his resignation, which Charles as often refused to accept, until Goring at last flatly refused to serve him any longer.

Now pressure was brought to bear on him to sever his connection with Clementina. The Earl Marischal, Cluny, Alexander Murray, even the failing Chevalier, besides his supporters in Scotland, begged him to 'put away' his entanglements.

In 1756 he had sunk so low in debauchery and need that he appealed for money to the French king whose pension he had refused in 1747. In 1760 James sent urgent appeals to his son to come and see him in Rome, but Charles always refused to visit the papal city. In the same year even Clementina fled from his conduct and his cruelty, taking Charlotte with her. Charles wrote on this event that 'I shall be in the greatest affliction until I get back the child which was my only comfort in my misfortunes,' but they sought refuge in a convent.

The prince had dismissed his secretary, Murray, as being implicated in this escape, and the latter wrote warning Charles that 'Your Royal Highness is resolved to destroy yourself' and that 'from being once the admiration of Europe you are now become the reverse'.

Poor Clementina, ever loving, wrote to her 'Dearest Prince' a touching letter of excuse for leaving him and begged him to save himself, saying that reports had reached her that he was not himself and that his head 'was quite gone'.

Cardinal York exerted himself to the utmost to induce his brother to visit his dying father and live in Rome. Charles replied through his secretary that he would never do so, but at last set out for Rome on the last day of 1765. It was too late, for James died on New Year's Day 1766, and the prince arrived in Rome only to find himself 'Charles III, by the Grace of God King of England, Scotland, France, and Ireland' but without land or country, friends or hope – poor prince! pitiful king!

He had one consolation – he was now reconciled to his 'dearest brother', who made over to him the whole of his pension from the pope. He retained for a time his late father's old secretary, Andrew Lumisden, Sir Robert Strange's brother-in-law, through whom Clementina tried to effect a reconciliation, but Charles was now too embittered to want her or his child and continued to console himself with drink, notwithstanding his frequent assertion of his kingly status. This led to a breach with Lumisden, who refused to drive with him in his coach because of his intoxicated condition, and the whole of his suite and Scots adherents were dismissed and replaced by 'one or two Italians'.

His thoughts now turned once again towards marriage and an heir to the 'throne' of Britain, so the weary hunt for a suitable princess, which had been the duty of his father after the 1715 rebellion, was repeated in that of his son with far less prospect of a suitable alliance. He went to Paris to further the scheme and had some sort of assistance from King Louis. Finally the consent of the Princess de Stolberg was obtained for a marriage with her daughter Louise, who was ambitious to be a 'queen', and the wedding took place in Ancona on 17 April 1772.

It was a most unhappy marriage. The pope still refused the longed-for royal honours. Clementina and her daughter were in Rome and making trouble, and although for a time the prince reformed his habits, by the next year they had again returned. In 1774 the royal couple moved to Florence, and there he was in correspondence with his daughter, Charlotte, threatening that he would 'give her up for ever if she thought of marriage'.

Here he was also at variance with his wife, who taunted him with his early rising habits and with 'not wishing to sleep more than five hours with a pretty young woman who loves you'.

In 1780 she left him for ever, eventually eloping with an Italian poet after a wretched scene in which Charles brutally attacked her – the last Stuart 'Queen of England'! She can scarcely be blamed for leaving her unhappy consort, but her conduct with the poet, Alfieri, even after she had been received into the household of her brother-in-law, the cardinal, for her protection, destroys any feeling of sympathy that she otherwise might have claimed.

Charles was now in rapidly failing health, an asthmatic and apoplectic old man. His dissolute habits had of necessity been abandoned, and, failing as he was, he at last did what he could to repair his faults. He legitimized his daughter, Charlotte, and created her 'Duchess of Albany', leaving her all his belongings in a will dated 23 March 1783. He was believed to be dying on that day and received the sacrament of the Church of Rome for the first time since his renunciation.

He recovered from his illness, however, and then began a desire to have his daughter at his side. She joined him in July 1784, a young woman whom Andrew Lang describes as tall, strong and good-humoured. He also says that Charles received her with delight, covered her with jewels and on St Andrew's Day invested her with the green ribbon of that Order.

She nursed him with great tenderness, 'checked him when he drank too much' and made friends with her uncle, the cardinal, who had hitherto refused to recognize her and had been offended at her legitimization.

At the end of 1785 Charles and his daughter returned to Rome from Florence but without any subsequent improvement in his health, and he died on the last day of January 1788. Charlotte followed him to the grave a few months later as the result of a fall from her horse.

Of the last survivor of the race of Stuart kings, Henry, Cardinal and Duke of York, there is little to relate. He had sunk his royal aspirations in his spiritual yearnings in 1749, when he accepted his cardinal's hat. Once a rich man, the French Revolution and subsequent wars of conquest swept all that away, and he was living in poverty in Venice in 1798 when his plight was communicated to George III of England, who had generously stated in 1785 that if the princes were ever in need it would be a real pleasure to assist them and who now came to the rescue and allowed the cardinal a pension of four thousand pounds a year.

In gratitude for this act of charity, Henry, in his will, bequeathed the crown jewels of England, taken to France in 1688 by James II, to the prince regent, later George IV. Henry died in 1807.

So ended the royal Stuarts – a history of thrilling events and stirring times through nearly five centuries, ending in poverty and charity, the 'Elector' and 'Usurper' of 1715 and 1745 coming to the rescue of the 'Pretender's' son and bestowing on him a pension that preserved him from need.

Of such a finale it may well be written that it conferred honour not on the giver or receiver alone but on both of them alike. Nor was this the only occasion upon which the royal house of Stuart was recognized and honoured in the last of its members by the reigning house of England, for it is said that when, in the early nineteenth century, Cardinal York paid a

187

visit to George, Prince Regent, doubtless with regard to his bequeathal of the crown jewels, the cardinal addressed him with all the regal dignity of his race, as from the superior to the inferior, by his Electoral title as 'Your Highness'. The 'First Gentleman in Europe' replied with the courtesy that had earned him his name, 'I beg Your Royal Highness to be seated.' A costless honour, an empty title, but a courtesy that must have been keenly appreciated by its recipient – if it really happened. Quite likely it is only one of the many romances, and the last of them, that the ages have woven around the Stuarts, as no one else was likely to be present at such a meeting between the prince regent of England and the aged cardinal. Be that as it may, it is a pleasant little fable with which to close the story of the last of the Stuarts.